An Apple a Day

An Apple a Day

Adventures
of a Country Doctor

by

CORNELIUS SLATER, M.D.

NEW YORK
THE VANGUARD PRESS

Library of Congress Cataloging-in-Publication Data

Slater, Cornelius, 1940-
An apple a day.

1. Slater, Cornelius, 1940-   . 2. Physicians—
England—East Anglia—Biography.   I. Title.
R489.S625A3   1987   610.924 [B]   87–25400
ISBN 0–8149–0932–9

To my wife and 'Timothy Bacon',
long-suffering partners both.

The stories in this book are based on the truth but names, places, times and circumstances are all false! The patients of the fictitious Tunford can lie in their beds safe in the knowledge that they do not appear. The only person they might remember from long ago, despite the heavy disguise given to him by the man he became, is the 'green' young doctor.

An Apple a Day

1

"He's a little sod, Doctor. He swears loike a bloody trooper," said Mrs. Pyman with a hint of pride in her voice. I looked at the little sod again and he gave me a gap-toothed smile. Tow haired, scruffy, freckle faced and cheeky, seven year old Tommy Pyman was a true product of his environment. Born into a farm labourer's family late in his mother's fertile years, he was the youngest of a family of six and was obviously picking up the language and habits of the rest of the clutch.

The young rebel had been brought to see me this morning because the schoolmaster had noticed a patch of impetigo on Tommy's cheek and had referred him to the doctor forthwith. The referal had been timely because Mrs. Pyman had been treating the infection with applications of vaseline and it had been spreading rapidly. But a few treatments with an antibiotic ointment woud soon cure it.

"Oh, he swears does he?" I said in mock surprise, trying hard to suppress my amusement at Mrs. Pyman's own slip of the tongue.

"Well, I'm afraid I'm going to make you swear too, Mrs. Pyman, because you'll have to keep him off school with that."

Mrs. Pyman rolled her eyes to the ceiling in pretence of horror at the prospect.

"Must Oi?" she asked.

"Yes," I replied. "The master's right. That is impetigo and we don't want it all over the school. The ointment I'm going to give you should get it better fairly soon, but he must have a separate bar of soap and towel from everyone else in the house so that it doesn't go round the rest of you."

"Whatever yew say," said Mrs. Pyman.

From the tone of her voice I doubted that my advice about

the soap and towel would be followed, but I wrote out a prescription for some Neomycin ointment, handed it to Tommy's mother and asked her to bring him back to see me at the end of the week.

As the Pymans left and I pressed the buzzer for the next patient I wondered, for the umpteenth time this past month, if this really was the job for me. I had been qualified in medicine for three years now and until a few months ago I had expected that my life would be spent as a 'proper doctor' in a hospital. Practically the whole of my training had been geared to that end because the teaching hospital consultants from whom I had learned most of what I knew about my craft had encouraged their pupils to be like themselves. To these 'great men' general practitioners were very definitely the failures of the medical profession who deserved only a measure of condescending sympathy for having fallen off the consultant ladder. And here I was, a one time aspiring consultant surgeon, suffering the shock and ignominy of having become a specimen of that lowest form of medical life, the much mocked and reviled general practitioner.

My decision to go into general practice had been caused by the realisation that to become a hospital consultant would take another ten years of low pay, hard work, examinations and scruffy little furnished flats in and around London. When I had been single that prospect hadn't been too frightening, but just over a year ago I had married my wife Frances, who had been a staff nurse at my old teaching hospital. Three months later Frances had become pregnant (our baby daughter was now three months old) and it was in the middle of the pregnancy that the thought of putting my family through the hardship of being dependent on an aspiring consultant had bitten deep into my conscience. The only thing for it seemed to be to go into general practice where the pay was better in the early years and there was certainly far more security.

But after one month in the job I felt I could easily have

answered the consultant's wife who had once said to me, "Do please tell me Dr. Slater. What on earth do general practitioners do?" The reply seemed to be, "Treat coughs, colds and spotty-faced kids."

Several times recently it had come into my mind that if I had never passed the 'eleven plus', never gone to grammar school and then to medical school in London, I might have been perfectly happy as a plumber in the small northern industrial town where I had spent my childhood.

But despite my general gloom there was just one consolation. At least we now lived in the country, and that was a big plus to set against all the professional minuses.

When we had come in August to look Tunford had seemed absolutely idyllic. Set in the midst of rich, rolling farmland in the heart of East Anglia, the village's main street was lined with ancient half-timbered houses which sweltered in the heat and seemed to have a sleepy timeless quality. Cats dozed on doorsteps and hardly a breath of air moved. The peace and tranquillity had been broken only by the sound of cricket ball on willow, punctuated by bursts of desultory clapping, coming from the general direction of the cricket meadow. The atmosphere of the place had been enthralling, and Frances and I had been totally captivated by this vision of unspoiled rural England in late summer.

It was perhaps as well that we had seen what Tunford could be like at its best because now it was November and the place looked very different. The fields around the village which had previously been covered with ripening corn were now ploughed brown and bare. The wind howled, and it seemed to rain every day. Lorries loaded with sugar-beet thundered monotonously down the main street from dawn until dusk and there was mud everywhere — even splattered on the windows of some of the houses. It seemed incredible that summer's beauty could have turned into this.

But if the change in the village environment was a shock, at least my new boss, Dr. Timothy Bacon, hadn't altered one bit. At the interview which he had given Frances and me back in August I had liked him immensely, despite the obvious differences in our backgrounds. For whereas I was a working class lad who could be said to have done well, he was a fully paid-up member of the English middle class. A sincere man in his early thirties he had very gentlemanly public school manners, but he also had a very dry sense of humour. And I had rightly judged that he was a hard worker who wouldn't be one to fob off his work onto his assistant while he spent the afternoons on the golf course. Although he was still a bachelor, he lived like a Saxon thane in a huge wisteria-covered house right in the middle of Tunford. His household was managed by a bustling middle-aged housekeeper called Mrs. Yallop whose cooking was a legend in the county, and altogether the life of a country doctor, as lived by Dr. Bacon, had seemed, back in the summer, to be far more comfortable, elegant and secure than I could have imagined. How pleasant, I had thought, to live like Timothy Bacon in such beautiful surroundings, to meander on one's visits along leafy lanes, to know all the country people and be universally respected. Unrushed, dignified, close to nature, satisfying; that is how it had seemed three months ago. And it was the mirage of such an existence which had brought me to East Anglia in pleasant anticipation.

But the reality of life as a general practitioner was very different. In my first month I had had endless calls to children with snotty noses, earaches and coughs, old people with social problems, and neurotics whose only real problem was boredom. I had had very little chance indeed to practise the high-powered scientifically-based medicine for which I had been trained. There was no doubt that it was the frustration and disappoint-ment of my first plunge into the cold water of general practice which had started me thinking bitterly that I might as well have been a plumber. Plumbers at least had an opportunity to use their training to the full and there seemed to be a lot of job-satisfaction in their trade. Mending burst pipes and repairing leaky stop-cocks sounded a great deal more worthwhile than treating impetigo.

But my reverie was interrupted as my next patient walked into the room. A ruddy-faced old countryman, he looked the picture of health.

"Oi got a push on me arm and it's wholly suing," he announced before I could even say hello. My mind went completely blank for a moment. I hadn't a clue what he was talking about. He might as well have addressed me in Norwegian, but I realised it would have been instant defeat to admit it.

"Well, could you please take your shirt off and pop on the couch so that I can examine you," I said as soon as I had recovered my wits.

He did as he was told. His jacket came off quite quickly, but then he very gingerly undid the buttons of his open-necked shirt and slowly eased the garment off. The problem was exposed. He had a large suppurating boil on his left upper arm, and in my mind I was now able to translate his sentence. "Push" must equal boil and "suing" festering. "Wholly" probably meant really.

I reflected that even if I hadn't done anything terribly exciting that morning, at least I had learnt three new words.

2

"Can Oi speak ter the doctor, please?" said the caller.

"He's off duty. What do you want him for?" replied Frances in tones far softer than the words appear in print.

"Me woife's runned out of her tablets."

"Well, I'm afraid the doctor's out," said my wife as emphatically as she could.

The practice was a dispensing one and the patients seemed to expect a twenty-four hour repeat prescription service from the young doctor living over the shop. To our accommodation-starved London eyes the flat over the surgery which went with my job had seemed marvellous at first, but in a few short weeks we had learned some of its disadvantages, continual knockers-at-the-door being one of them.

The business premises of the practice were in a very attractive looking thatched cottage right opposite Timothy's house and handily next door to the fish and chip shop. The part of the surgery building set aside as a flat was tiny but so, it had to be admitted, was the rent we paid to my boss for the privilege of living there. Our quarters consisted of two bedrooms and a bathroom upstairs with a small kitchen, sitting room and dining room squashed round at the back of the practice dispensary downstairs. We had our own separate front entrance from the street but the back door led only into a minute garden enclosed by a high wall.

I had very quickly become paranoid about answering the front door when I was off duty and had decided to behave like most other married GPs and use my wife as a shield. Frances tried very hard to do her stuff, but the girl I had married just wasn't cut out to be the dragon at the gate. Her little white lie about me being out, for instance, was just about to go sadly wrong.

"What d'yer mean he's out?" said the patient accusingly. "Oi can see his car in the street there." It was inconceivable to him that I could be out for a walk or perhaps even riding a bicycle. He obviously believed that doctors should either be sitting behind their desks in the surgery or right next to the telephone in their homes. When they were not thus employed they had to be out on their rounds in their cars.

Anyway, Frances didn't think of making up more excuses. There stood our old Morris in the street and it seemed absolute proof of her guilt.

"Er yes," said Frances. "So it is." And to add to my wife's acute embarrassment just at this moment I walked out of the sitting room with a newspaper in my hand. I was in full view of the front door.

"Oh, there you are, Corney," said Frances blushing. "Did you come in the back way?"

"What back way?" I asked, puzzled. Then I caught sight of her crimson face and the penny dropped at last.

"Hello, Mr. Felgate. What is it?" I said, taking over the situation and inwardly cursing myself for not keeping well out of sight. Frances dived past me to go and hide her confusion in the kitchen.

"Moi woife's runned out of her tablets," he repeated.

Unlike Timothy Bacon I wasn't yet a walking encyclopaedia of all the patients in the practice but I did know the Felgates. Any doctor who had been in the Tunford practice for more than a week would have done, because the Felgates were what is known in the trade as 'senders'. Mrs. Felgate was a diabetic, it was true, but it was of the mild maturity-onset type, controlled by tablets and diet. Most of the visits which she requested were on account of trivial things which could well have been dealt with in the surgery if she would have asked one of her many relatives to bring her along in a car. But she found it far more convenient to call the doctor out to her home in Garham and then send her poor long suffering husband cycling the three

15

miles up to the Tunford surgery to pick up whatever medication had been prescribed (or 'described' as she would put it). The constant cycling helped to keep Mr. Felgate fit however, for unlike his wife, who was fat and sluggish, he was thin and wirey and looked a good ten years younger than his sixty summers.

"It is Sunday afternoon, you know, Mr. Felgate. Couldn't you have called up to the surgery yesterday morning when the dispensary was open?" I said as severely as I could.

"Oi was workin' then," he replied unrepentantly. I hadn't any quick reply to that because Mr. Felgate was Garham's gravedigger. As far as I knew I hadn't been the cause of his Saturday morning labours but he had a sort of accusing look about him as though I had and I didn't pursue the matter.

"You've tried Dr. Bacon, have you? He's on duty," I said.

"Yes, an' Mrs. Yallop says he's out," replied Mr. Felgate. "His car ain't there anyway," he added wickedly.

"All right," I sighed. "Just wait here till I get my keys."

It was obvious that Mrs. Felgate should have her diabetic tablets but nevertheless it was extremely annoying to be caught like this when I was supposed to be off duty. I went back into the sitting room and found my bunch of keys in the pocket of my discarded jacket which was draped over the back of an armchair. Unfortunately there was no communicating door between our flat and the dispensary, so I had to go out into the street and round to the main surgery door to open up. This in itself was a risky business when I was off duty, because, even in my few weeks' experience I had found that people seemed to appear from nowhere when the doors were opened. The problem was at its worst after dusk when the lights seemed to attract patients like moths. But fortunately this afternoon only Mr. Felgate followed me as I unlocked the door and went into the waiting room.

Some people would have called the Tunford practice's waiting room quaint, but I took a more jaundiced view. On a Sunday afternoon it was quiet and empty, of course, but during business hours it was far too small for the number of people who crammed into it. The light from the two small circular windows was poor, and with the low dark-beamed ceiling and rows of wooden benches usually packed with suffering humanity a strong impression was created of what it must have been like on the lower gun deck of Nelson's 'Victory' two hours after the battle of Trafalgar. In cold weather this impression was heightened by the acrid sulphur dioxide fumes which blew back from the small and inefficient coke heating stove whenever the wind was in the wrong direction — and it usually was. When the place was in full swing our receptionist, Mrs. Runbelow, sat behind a desk in a corner diagonally opposite the stove answering the telephone, making appointments and filing notes in the ancient metal filing cabinet which stood behind her. There was no pretence at any privacy. Unless they were very deaf, everyone in the waiting room could hear both sides of every telephone conversation. And because the wall between the waiting room and the two tiny consulting rooms was paper thin, the same rule applied to consultations with the doctors.

But it was all hallowed by long tradition and at least the entertainment provided by all these distractions did away with the necessity to put out glossy magazines to read.

Our consulting rooms were like the waiting room, in that they contained only the bare essentials and would probably have been condemned by any self respecting Public Health inspector. Nevertheless, in these primitive surroundings we lanced boils, sutured wounds and removed sebaceous cysts with the minimum of aseptic precautions. The opportunities for cross-infection must have been rife, but only very rarely did clean wounds become infected; for the most part bacteria and patients seemed to live with one another in cheerful harmony.

Fortunately the same sort of relationship was rapidly developing between Timothy Bacon and myself. Our characters were very different, he quiet and reserved with the patience of Job, I definitely more brash and inclined to show my temper.

17

But the difference in temperament may have been the reason why we were settling down so well together. I greatly respected my colleague as a doctor. He was very conscientious and had an immense knowledge of his patients and their families. He seemed to thoroughly enjoy just dealing with people and was rarely nettled by their cussedness. Guided by him I was slowly beginning to learn that there was indeed pleasure and satisfaction to be had in general practice if you became interested in the patient and not just his disease.

But on this particular Sunday afternoon I wasn't too interested in Mr. Felgate, Mrs. Felgate, or any of the diseases they might have had in the past twenty years. I took Mrs. Felgate's empty tablet bottle from her husband's grubby hand, and, telling him to stay in the waiting room, I stalked into the dispensary and shut the door firmly behind me.

Here there was peace. With its rows of neatly labelled bottles on the shelves round the walls and its slightly 'hospital' smell, the dispensary reminded me of the biochemistry laboratory back at medical school and to go in there was for me like a return to the womb. It was tiny, just as every other room in the building was tiny, but Mr. Somerville the dispenser kept it in apple-pie order. I had no trouble at all in finding the stock bottle for Mrs. Felgate's chlorpropamide tablets, and my temper had evaporated by the time I had counted out a month's supply into the patient's container. I made a note of the prescription on a notepad on the dispensary bench and then handed the goods to Mr. Felgate through the small sliding hatch in the door.

"Thank yew," he said without much grace.

"OK," I replied. "But mind you come in surgery hours next time. We employ a dispenser to hand out pills you know."

"Oi'll try," he said, but in a tone which made me think I hadn't been tough enough. As he marched out triumphantly I put the stock bottle back in its place on the shelf and started locking up, muttering to myself as I did so. It really was too much the way people treated us. I bet if they had to pay they wouldn't behave like that. But then if people had to pay they would hardly have flocked to the Tunford surgery! I stopped and looked around the empty waiting room. The whole set-up was really dreadfully scruffy and inadequate. Why, there wasn't even a lavatory in the place. Patients were always getting taken short in the surgery and I was forever directing them round to our flat and the upstairs bathroom. It was a time-consuming procedure which pleased nobody.

But I smiled when I thought of an incident two days before when a young wife had walked into my consulting room with a look of consternation on her face.

"Chroist boy," she said. "Oi could do with a pee."

"Oh dear," I said, beginning to get up from my chair. "The only loo is in the flat upstairs. I'll show you up there if you like."

"Naaw, tha's orl roight," she replied, knowing how busy I was. "Let's get this over first. There's plenty of hedges on the way hoom."

3

Timothy pointed with his pen.

"I think you'd better do this visit, Corney," he said as we both surveyed the call book spread open on the kitchen table. It was just after morning surgery and whenever possible the two of us had a brief meeting and a cup of coffee in Timothy's kitchen at this time of day. Standing or sitting in front of the large Aga cooker to warm our hands and feet we would exchange news and sort out the visits while Mrs. Yallop bustled discreetly in the background. It was only a brief respite from the hurly burly of our work but I think we both looked forward to it. Come to think of it I expect Mrs. Yallop did too, but although she no doubt picked up a few snippets of gossip she was good at holding her tongue and we trusted her.

"Why the Pendleton girl?" I asked. "Don't you usually go there?"

Timothy blushed and Mrs. Yallop made as if she hadn't heard by banging some pans around in the scullery.

"Well, I don't think she's very ill," said my colleague as he swirled the dregs of his coffee round in the bottom of his cup examining them over-closely before he drained the vessel. "You shouldn't have any problem in dealing with her."

But his blush and the careful avoidance of a straight look in my direction hinted at the real reason why Timothy didn't want to go. His unerring nose had smelled a trap. For to every matron in the district who had an eligible unmarried daughter it seemed a mortal sin that T.J. Bacon hadn't been hooked yet, and they had been hunting him remorselessly since he had arrived in Tunford three years before.

Mrs. Pendleton was one of the more persistent huntresses and I gathered from my colleagues's blush that she must have reopened hostilities in her longstanding battle to make a match between Timothy and her daughter Elizabeth. Personally, I thought that Elizabeth was very attractive, but I suppose it was the daunting Mrs. Pendleton who was her daughter's worst enemy.

"O.K. I'll go," I said, thinking how uncomplicated life was when you were married. But then, even if I hadn't been, I doubted whether my scuffed shoes and direct northern manner would have made me the most sought after man in Tunford. If five years at a London medical school had taught me anything, it was where I stood with eligible females.

Half an hour later I drove up to the front of the Pendleton house on the outskirts of the village. Mr. Pendleton was a bank manager in Angleton, the nearest town, and on the one or two occasions I had met him I hadn't much liked him. He was too unbending and self-important for my taste.

The house was a very pleasant Georgian building but the garden, I thought, totally reflected Mr. Pendleton's character. Very formal, with neatly clipped, fussy little privet hedges, it looked as if it had been laid out by a municipal parks director. With what I thought was very poor taste the kitchen garden had been separated from the rose beds with some ghastly white-painted ranch type fencing which looked completely out of place in such a rural setting. But to my mind the worst abomination of all was an old fashioned town gas lamp which had been painted cream and green, electrified, and stuck in the middle of the front lawn to act as an outside light. It was a commuter's garden if ever there was one.

I climbed out of my car and walked up to the front door. Near the knocker, where you couldn't miss it, a small note had been pinned. It read, 'Timothy — sorry I had to go out, Elizabeth upstairs. Please go right in — Monica P.'

Well, I thought, that would have annoyed Dr. Bacon for a start. I don't think he regarded himself as being on Christian name terms with the Pendletons — quite the opposite, in fact.

I shrugged my shoulders, pushed open the door and walked into the hall. Noting some ornamental ducks flighting their way up one wall of the stairs, I followed them.

"Hello. Where are you?" I called as I reached the landing.

"In here," replied a forlorn but somehow sexy voice.

I pushed open the door of the bedroom from whence I thought the sound had come and there she was. What a dish! Elizabeth Pendleton was sitting up in bed with a copy of 'Vogue' on her lap. As befitted a sophisticate of twenty-five her make-up had been expertly applied and her glossy black hair had been so well groomed that you would have thought she was expecting a photographer from 'Paris Match' rather than the doctor. She didn't look desperately ill. That is, she didn't until she saw who had walked in. The welcoming smile froze on her lips and she gave a little cough. Funny how some people always do that when they see a doctor.

"Oh, it's you," she said, with a look of distaste. "I was expecting Dr. Bacon."

"Well, he's busy today so I'm afraid you'll have to make do with me," I said, trying hard not to say anything ambiguous. Perhaps I already had?

"What's the trouble?"

"I've got a sore throat and Mummy insisted I should see the doctor."

"How long have you had it?"

"Two or three days," she answered with a blush.

"I gather you have a cough. Are you bringing any sputum up?"

"No."

"Any wheeze?"

"No."

"OK. Open your mouth and say 'Ah'," I said as I reached for my pen torch. All my inspection revealed was a fine set of pearly white teeth and a normal looking pharynx.

"Hmm," I murmured non-committally. I took her pulse rate. It was normal. I bet if she had taken mine it would have

22

been a hundred and forty a minute. But I tried not to betray the fact.

"Right, I'd better listen to your chest," I said.

"You don't want me to take my nightie off, do you?" she said with a look of horror in her eyes.

"Er no, I don't think that will be necessary," I stammered. And it wasn't. Elizabeth's nightdress didn't leave much to the imagination. I took my stethoscope out of my jacket pocket, applied the earpieces to my ears and placed the listening bell on the lower slopes of my patient's right breast.

"Take some big breaths," I said. Thank God I hadn't followed the recent fashion for very short stethoscope tubing. At least with the outmoded instrument I had had since I was a student I was able to keep a decent distance from the temptress by dint of two and a half feet of rubber piping. But nevertheless, as her bosom heaved I caught a whiff of some exotic perfume and I felt a cold sweat breaking out on my brow. I quickly moved the stethoscope bell over to the other side of her chest. There wasn't a single extraneous squeak.

I unplugged my ears, stepped back and returned the instrument to my pocket.

"Absolutely clear," I said. "I don't think you need much in the way of treatment. Take a couple of aspirins if you get feverish and drink plenty of fluids. There's no need to stay in bed either. You can get up this afternoon."

I think Elizabeth had realised that I was nervous. She agreed to obey my instructions and then watched me coolly as I backed out of the room like an anxious courtier. I said goodbye at the door, turned, and fled down the stairs as if I were being chased by a jealous husband.

It was only when I was a quarter of a mile down the road in my car that I recovered enough to slap myself on the thigh and roar with laughter.

I could hardly wait to see Timothy again, but it was lunch-time before I finished the rest of my visits and arrived back in

Tunford. Timothy was just climbing out of his car when I drew up outside the surgery. I waved to him and he waited on the pavement until I joined him.

"I can see why you sent me there," I said with a grin like a sliced melon on my face.

He smiled.

"Did she stroke your arm then?" he asked.

"No, but . . ."

"Well you're a lucky boy then, aren't you," he said enigmatically, and without another word he stumped off across the street to his front door.

*

Calls like the one to Elizabeth Pendleton certainly made me glad that I was safely married, but one of the things which made me quite unreasonably jealous of Timothy was the knowledge that the women of the practice were always naming their babies after him. I tried hard to persuade myself that this was solely because he was still a bachelor (and therefore a figure of romance), but in my more sober moments I realised that it was more likely to be my rugged countenance which put the mothers off.

Old Nurse Parmenter, the midwife, who was close to retirement, maintained, as she had done all her working life, that obstetrics was women's work and that general practitioners (especially male general practitioners) shouldn't interfere. She strongly objected to us attending all our booked home confinements, but, although she did all she could to dissuade us, we regularly turned up to supervise the delivery of our patients' babies. Sometimes the atmosphere in the labour room was so frosty you almost needed an ice-axe to break through to the mother-to-be. But despite the midwife's hostility both Timothy and I stuck to our guns and kept going to our ladies because we knew that, if a woman had a haemorrhage or a newborn baby needed resuscitating, it was far better for the doctor to be actually on the spot when the emergency occurred than snoring in his bed five miles away. Nine times out of ten everything would be normal, of course, and the midwife would pour scorn on us for worrying, but we knew we were right and most of the mothers deeply appreciated our presence. Although we were always strictly deferential to Nurse Parmenter to her face, we told each other many a well-embellished story about her during our morning coffee-breaks in front of Timothy's kitchen range. For despite her claims to competence, the old girl was certainly slowing up. Blaming this not so much on her obesity as on her addiction to tea and cigarettes, we reckoned she couldn't move a limb without her intake of caffeine and nicotine.

We invented a recurring scene of what happened every time Nurse Parmenter was called at night. First she would have to have a ten minute cough and spit session, then encase herself in three layers of corsets, smoke a cigarette and down at least two cups of tea before she left her bungalow. And while she was going through this routine the mother-to-be might well have progressed to being a mother-in-fact. Although a B.B.A. (born before arrival) case would have been thought a disgrace by most midwives, Nurse Parmenter didn't get very agitated about it at all. She seemed to think that most babies dropped out pretty normally anyway, so what did it matter if she was occasionally a few minutes late? We were always beating her to it, but she didn't appear to notice when we made pointed remarks about the unreliability of telephones these days or asked solicitously whether her ancient Austin was still in good working order.

Mind you, I had my own problems with the telephone. I absolutely hated answering the thing in the middle of the night, and when the bell of our bedside extension jangled in my ear at four o'clock one foggy morning I cursed like a trooper as I searched for the light switch. But the curse died from my lips when I realised who the call was from. It was Edward Crabbe from Kingtree whose wife Vera was expecting a baby.

"Moi woife's started, Doctor," he announced. "An' the pains are comin' every foive minutes."

"All right, Mr. Crabbe," I said. "I'll be along as soon as I can. Did you let the midwife know?"

"Yes, some toime agew. She should be 'ere soon."

"Good," I said. "Won't be long."

I replaced the receiver and dressed hurriedly. This was Mrs. Crabbe's third pregnancy. The two previous babies had been born without any complications but nevertheless I always obeyed the old maxim that whenever a doctor is called to a midwifery case he should go straightaway. Then if he arrives at the woman's bedside and finds some disaster has occurred, he cannot blame himself afterwards for not hurrying.

Within twenty minutes of the telephone call I was pulling up in the Crabbe's farmyard four, seemingly endless, foggy miles from Tunford. An outside light attached high on the corner of the house dimly illuminated the scene and I noted that the midwife's car was nowhere in sight. I took my midwifery bag from the car boot and marched the few steps to the partially open kitchen door. A woman in her sixties (from the family likeness Mrs. Crabbe's mother imported for the occasion) got up from a chair and smiled at me as I pushed the door open.

"Hello, Doctor," she said. "Oi think yew're just in toime. Go straight up will yew."

She indicated a door which led to the stairs. I went through it and met Mr. Crabbe who was halfway down the flight. A short, dark, tubby man he looked more like the owner of a Greek restaurant than an East Anglian farmer. But he was very much a native, and was normally as phlegmatic as the rest of the breed. Just at this moment, though, he seemed to be in quite a stew.

"Thank God yew got here," he said. "We sent for the mid-woife an hour ago. The old bugger's still not come an' moi woife wants to push."

"Right, lead on!" I said, with some urgency in my voice. As always on these occasions I was trying hard to maintain a professional veneer of confidence, but inwardly my pulse was racing and my knees were like water.

He turned back up the stairs and I followed him to his wife's bedroom.

I liked Mrs. Crabbe. She seemed to be a good mother and was happy and content to be the wife of a small farmer, looking after her few hens and making jams for the Women's Institute. She wasn't a desperate beauty, but as an uncle of mine used to say of a homely wife who was one of his neighbours, 'She's a good cook. What more could any man want?' What indeed — a good cook is worth a lot to a man.

But right now cooking wasn't the foremost subject on Mrs. Crabbe's mind. She was sitting in her nightdress on the edge of the bed with her hands on her stomach and a wincing look of pain on her face. As I came in the pain seemed to ease off a little and she gave me a little smile.

"Hello, Doctor," she said. "Oi think it's nearly here."

I thought so too. Her husband was frothing over with agitation behind me, so to relieve the tension a bit I turned and said, "Can you get me a bowl of hot water, some soap and lots of old newspapers, please Mr. Crabbe."

"Certainly," he said and bustled out. He looked relieved to be able to do something.

As he went off I asked Mrs. Crabbe to lie back on the bed so that I could examine her. The baby was lying head first, just as it had at the last ante-natal appointment five days before. And with my stethoscope I was able to detect a good strong foetal heart. The membranes had ruptured and the liquor was clear. In short, everything seemed to be progressing normally.

I was just thinking about doing a vaginal examination to assess how far labour had progressed, when there was another firm contraction of the uterine muscle. Mrs. Crabbe made a little whimpering noise and then clenched her teeth and gripped my arm tightly. As the contraction reached its maximum intensity I caught a glimpse of the baby's head on the mother's

27

perineum. The head retreated again as the pain subsided, but nevertheless I knew now that we wouldn't have to wait very long.

"I saw the baby's head that time," I said. "When you get a pain again could you hold your breath and really push down into your tail."

Mrs. Crabbe smiled at me and nodded. I used the interval between pains to rush to the bedroom door and shout down the stairs for that bowl of water and the newspapers.

Mr. Crabbe delivered the articles to the labour room very quickly but he was gone again as rapidly as he had come. It was patently obvious he didn't want to stay to see his infant born, and I didn't blame him one bit. When you've worked on a farm and seen vets struggling with calving ropes it doesn't do your obstetric imagination any good at all.

Another pain came and Mrs. Crabbe gave a good strong push just as I had told her to. I feverishly unpacked some of my kit from my obstetric bag, put on my plastic apron and washed my hands in the bowl of water which Mr. Crabbe had placed on the dressing table. All the time I kept an anxious eye on the baby's head as it slowly expanded the mother's vulva. I barely had time to complete my preparations when, with the next pain, a perfect but rather small male infant came bawling into the world, straight on to a copy of the Eastern Daily News which I had put between Mrs. Crabbe's legs. Not very sterile, you might think, (though there are those who say that there is nothing as sterile as that particular publication). Anyway, the sheets were saved.

"It's a boy," I said between sucks, as I aspirated the infant's nasal passages clear of mucus with a small plastic mouth sucker which I had for the purpose.

"Is he normal, Doctor?"

"Looks like it," I said. I would do a full examination later.

Mrs. Crabbe sobbed softly with relief and joy as I clamped the umbilical cord with two Spencer Wells forceps and then with scissors divided the cord between the clamped instruments. As I did this I remembered the palaver Nurse Parmenter always made about catching the few drops of blood which exuded from the ends of the cord when she cut it. She would always dab the severed ends with cotton wool, which seemed an absolutely ludicrous thing to do when there was so much blood and amniotic fluid around the place anyway. This time the custom wasn't observed, but I did wipe some of the mess from the infant's eyes before I wrapped him in a small soft sheet made ready for the purpose and handed him to his mother to hold.

Mrs. Crabbe took him with a radiant smile on her face and for a few moments this little homely farmer's wife was the Madonna with her child. The miracle had happened again. For the doctor, however, the miracle wasn't quite over. Not until the placenta was out, because it is during this stage of labour, the third stage, that there is always a risk of a sudden catastrophic haemorrhage. But there weren't any complications. After a few minutes I delivered the placenta normally and with minimal blood loss. I rescued my Spencer Wells forceps from the maternal end of the umbilical cord and when I had made sure that the afterbirth was complete I wrapped it up in several sheets of newspaper and·put it down by the bed. If Mr. Crabbe was a follower of tradition he would later bury it in his rosebed.

Just as I was congratulating myself that Mrs. Crabbe wouldn't need any stitches I heard a car pull up in the yard outside. A few moments before I would have been oblivious to any external noise because of my anxiety over the delivery, but now I had obviously relaxed enough to allow extraneous noises to impinge upon my consciousness again.

"That will be Nurse Parmenter," I said, and Mrs. Crabbe smiled. What we had just been through together had made us friends and conspirators. I carried on collecting up my instruments until the midwife burst into the room like an anticyclone. The baby's father dragged along in her wake like an irrelevant piece of flotsam. But it was the flotsam I addressed when I said, "It's a boy." Mr. Crabbe grinned with delight and almost did a little dance in his pleasure. Nurse Parmenter's exertion in climbing the stairs had made her wheeze and she was very out of breath. At this hour in the morning she never looked her best but now her round and bespectacled face was white and pinched with suppressed fury.

"Good evening, Nurse," I said cheerfully. "Everything's normal and under control, I'm glad to say."

"'morning," she corrected me savagely between wheezes. Somehow I got the impression that she wasn't pleased at being beaten to it this time. I couldn't think why. It had all happened before. Perhaps she had been on the mat at county headquarters on account of all her B.B.A.s?

I turned back to Mrs. Crabbe. "By the way. What are you going to call him?" I asked.

"Well, Oi hadn't thought, Doctor," she replied. "Oi was expectin' a girl. That's what Dr. Bacon told me it would be when yew were away."

I laughed. Timothy had this little game he played in which he would tell the expectant ladies they were going to have whatever sex of child they most wanted. And whichever sex he told them he wrote down the opposite in the notes. If he were right with his guess the mothers would be delighted. However if he were wrong and taxed about it he would look in his notes and say, "Boy? Are you sure? Look, I wrote down girl here in the notes." The ploy had given him quite a reputation as a soothsayer, but this time he wasn't here to continue the game. And anyway, Mrs. Crabbe was now a Dr. Slater fan. I could hardly believe my ears when she looked at me and asked, "What's your first name, Doctor?"

"Cornelius," I replied proudly, and stretched myself up to my full height. As I did so I caught sight of myself in the dressing table mirror. Perhaps I wasn't such a bad looking chap after all?

"Cornelius," repeated Mrs. Crabbe slowly and thoughtfully. "Oi hadn't thought of that. Thank yew."

She looked at Mr. Crabbe and he winked and nodded his approval. It really was heady stuff for me, but I felt that poor

Nurse Parmenter was on the point of regurgitating the two cups of tea which she had undoubtedly consumed before she had left her bungalow. She didn't actually say anything, but she bustled round me clearing up the mess with such fervour that it seemed high time I went.

"Would you like a cup of tea, Doctor?" asked Mr. Crabbe. "No thanks," I said as I rinsed my hands again in the enamel basin on the dressing table. "I think I will be on my way, but I'm sure Nurse Parmenter would like a cup."

"Yes please," said the midwife, softening a little.

I dried my hands and before I packed my bag I took Mrs. Crabbe's blood pressure and felt her abdomen to make sure the uterus was well contracted. Everything was normal, so I gathered my instruments together as quickly as I could, anxious to be out of the new atmosphere in the bedroom as soon as possible. "Right," I said as I prepared to leave. "I'll see you later this morning, Mrs. Crabbe."

"Oh will you, Doctor?" she said. "Thank yew."

Then I bid them all goodbye and left. As I passed through the kitchen on the way to my car, Mrs. Crabbe's mother thanked me effusively for my efforts. Once again I was pressed to have a cup of tea and I graciously refused it in the same manner in which I shrugged off the praise. But although my demeanour appeared to be modest, inwardly I was lapping up the adulation like a half-starved cat at the milk bowl.

As I jumped into my car my spirits were soaring, and I drove off to Tunford and bed again in a really elated mood. When I got home I woke Frances and told her the good news. She didn't seem too interested, so I told her the story again at breakfast time. The response was still disappointing, but then I don't suppose it is that pleasant for a wife to have other women naming their children after her husband. Such subtleties were lost on me then though, and I wondered why she was so disinterested.

Later that morning I could hardly wait for surgery to end, and when it did and Timothy and I gathered for coffee, I wasted no time in telling him about the night's events. The name Cornelius Crabbe certainly had a ring to it and the more I repeated it the more I was pleased with myself. Timothy enjoyed the bit about Nurse Parmenter nearly vomiting her tea, but after a while he got sick of my gloating and tried to veer the conversation on to the rotten weather we were having and my bad luck being up half the night. But lack of sleep wasn't worrying me that morning, and I went on rubbing in my victory until my colleague became thoroughly bored, excused himself and sloped off on his visits.

And that might almost have been the end of the matter but for the fact that six weeks later the Crabbe baby's little pink registration card arrived in the surgery. I took out my pen and started to sign it, but as I did so my eyes nearly popped out of my head. To my utter dismay and consternation the Crabbes had chosen to call their dearly beloved third child, TIMOTHY CORNELIUS CRABBE.

4

"Git yer own dear," said Daisy from her chair when I walked into the Three Tuns one evening and asked her for a beer.

I did as I was told, collected a mug off one of the hooks in an alcove on the way to the cellar, and then went down the short flight of stone steps to draw off my pint straight from the wood. Although I had been warned that it was probably not a good thing for a doctor to be seen too frequently in the village pub, especially when he was new, the temptation of Daisy Woodcock's fine beer had been too great for me to resist for very long and I was now one of her accepted regulars.

The Three Tuns was a dull-looking building on the outside. Built during the last century in greyish coloured brick it had been rather neglected by the Brewers and the paintwork of the doors, windows and even the pub sign itself was faded and peeling. There was only one public room, which you entered directly from the street, and this had to serve as public bar, lounge bar and Daisy's living room all rolled into one. The pamment tiled floor was well worn, especially in front of the dart board where the two tiles adjacent to a brass distance marker let into the floor had been hollowed into a depression by the boots of the countless dart players who had stood there to take aim.

Wooden panelling, painted maroon, stretched halfway up the walls all round the room, and the originally cream paintwork of the upper walls and ceiling had been stained brown with nicotine, as had the lace curtains at the three small windows.

Some idea of the sort of person usually to be found in the place could be gained from back copies of the Racing Times and the Sunday Mirror which were scattered amongst the ash trays and beer mats on a couple of simple oak tables just inside the front door. But for the most part, of course, people didn't come to the pub to read. They sat on the wooden benches around the walls and drank their beer while Daisy held court from her armchair by the fire, the mantelpiece of which was bedecked with an interesting collection of dirty postcards.

Daisy Woodcock was what is usually known as 'a real character'. Now about sixty five, she had been keeping the pub single-handed since her husband had died fifteen years before. With curly grey hair, half spectacles on the end of her nose, floppy pink cardigan, grey skirt and slippers she would have passed for anyone's grandmother except perhaps for the cigarette which usually dangled from her lower lip and her frequent lapses into the vernacular. For Daisy had been used to dealing with men all her life and could swear with the best of them, although she knew very well how to suit her language according to the company. Absolute queen of her domain, she was a man's woman and didn't appreciate female company at all. In fact women were usually given pretty short shrift should they chance to drift into the pub. Daisy always said that the reason for this was that women had weak bladders; if they stayed too long they were sure to ask for the lavatory and she was ashamed to show them to her Elsan. But I suspected that the real reason was that the talk was always more muted when there were women about and Daisy didn't like that any more than did most of her customers.

In her youth Daisy had been a housemaid to Dr. Long, who had been in practice in Tunford during the twenties, and she was a recognised authority on village gossip, past and present. My chief delight was to go into the pub when there was nobody else there and sit opposite her while she yarned about the old days. I never tired of listening to her, even though I soon knew her repertoire.

One of her less savoury tales was of how a young girl had met 'a fate worse than death' in the boiler room of the church one night fifty years before. And another was how Slopsey Finch the poacher, having by mistake caught a cat in a snare one night, had skinned it and taken it to a customer in place of a promised rabbit. Apparently, he had later been thanked effusively for the young animal and asked to catch another if he could.

Slopsey was also the gentleman who one evening for a dare had swallowed a live mouse whole in front of the incredulous assembled company in the Three Tuns.

But more useful up to date information was frequently provided too and I often had an insight into what people had thought of the advice I had given them in the surgery. It wasn't all complimentary by any means. And as it turned out, it was to be another of the days when I was to hear some of the more deflating news.

I came up the steps from the cellar and sat down on one of the benches opposite the publican. We were alone. I handed Daisy a ten shilling note and she gave me the change from a pile of coins stacked on the mantelpiece next to her almost full glass of Guinness. I took a long pull of the delicious cool bitter.

"Ah, that's better," I said, when I had slaked my thirst. "And how are you, Mrs. Woodcock?"

"Oh, Oi'm all roight," said Daisy. "But thass a bloody good job fer yew, yew wasn't in here a few minutes agew."

"Why's that?" I asked.

"That Isaac Parr was in here."

At the mention of this name I stiffened slightly. It certainly was a good job I hadn't been there because Isaac and I had had words only that morning. The patient was a rotund, middle-aged worker from the sugar-beet factory in Angleton who was a little too fond of his beer. For several weeks I had been treating him for what I had at first regarded as genuine mild bronchitis, but as time had gone on I had come to consider that he was prolonging his illness in order to remain a gentleman of leisure at the taxpayers' expense. After a little altercation during my morning surgery, I had signed him off as fit to work the following day.

"Well, what did he say?" I asked.

"Cor, moi lad, yew're name was mud, Oi can tell yew. He say 'That bloody quack. He's signed me orf. And me coughed up blood this mornin'. He ranted and raved for over an hour, but that didn't stop him drinking four pints of moi best. Oi reckon yew did roight. He's a silly old sod, that he is."

Before I had come into the pub my opinion of Isaac had been the same as Daisy's, but now I wasn't so sure. I wasn't surprised that he had been cursing me to the skies, but I hadn't heard anything about coughing blood before. Really though, when I thought about it, I had pounced on him so hard that morning I hadn't given him a chance to say more than a word or two.

"Coughed up blood?" I said. "First I heard of it."

"Well now yew hev," said Daisy. "Don't expect it was much. Now how's that woife and daughter of yours?"

"Oh, both blossoming, thanks Mrs. Woodcock," I replied, and the conversation continued away from the subject of Isaac Parr's symptoms. But I didn't forget. Spitting blood sounded serious and the possible diagnoses which sprang to mind were pulmonary tuberculosis and cancer of the lung. I had a pleasant hour or so in the Three Tuns but even as I was walking home I couldn't get Isaac's problem (or rather my problem of how to deal with my patient in the light of new evidence) out of my mind. I mulled it over for the rest of the evening and it gave me a sleepless night too. But by the time I was behind my desk the next morning I had decided what to do. I wrote a letter to Isaac and got one of his neighbours, who chanced to attend surgery that morning, to pop it through the Parrs' letter box.

The note read as follows.

Dear Mr. Parr,
   I was looking through your records today and I noted that during your recent illness I didn't order a routine chest X-ray. For the sake of completeness I think this would be a good idea. If you agree perhaps you could take the enclosed request form to the X-ray Department at the Angleton General on any weekday between 9 a.m. and 4 p.m. Perhaps you could then come and see me about three days later for the result?
  I must stress that, although I am suggesting this investigation, my opinion of your fitness to work is likely to remain the same.
       Yours sincerely,

      C. Slater

It was only two days later that I received the chest X-ray report from Angleton. To my utter horror it read —
 'Large shadow seen in the right upper zone. This could be a carcinoma. Suggest referral to Chest Clinic for further investigations.'
 I was consumed with guilt which I tried not to show when Isaac came to see me the following evening.
 "I'm very much afraid there's a shadow in your right lung," I said.
 "Is it cancer?"
 "I don't know," I replied truthfully. "But that's one of the things we have to exclude. We'll get on with it as soon as possible. I'll arrange for an urgent appointment with the chest specialist and in the meantime you'd better go back on the club. I'm very sorry about this, but I really did think you were better."
 "Tha's orl roight, Doctor," replied an ashen faced Isaac. The

stuffing had been completely knocked out of him.

I explained that after Isaac had seen the specialist he could expect to be admitted to hospital within a very few days for some tests. As I talked I quietly gave a sigh of relief that he was taking it all so well. After all, he could have been very stroppy indeed considering the brusque way in which I had treated him before, but he meekly accepted the certificate which I gave him and left the surgery with a glum look on his face and not a trace of his old cockiness.

The very next day I did as I had promised and telephoned to fix up an urgent appointment for my patient with the chest specialist. Within a week Isaac had been admitted to the Regional Thoracic Centre and put through the investigatory mill. He turned up in the surgery the day after his discharge and from the moment he walked in I could see it was the old jaunty Isaac again.

"It's not cancer, Doc," he announced as he handed me the small buff envelope containing the discharge note.

"Thank God for that," I said as I tore the envelope open and glanced through the short letter inside.

It appeared that the shadow had been due to a patch of inflammation only and it should respond to the course of antibiotics which the hospital doctor had already prescribed.

I really was very relieved and pleased that I hadn't made too much of a mess of things after all. Isaac was pleased too. For one thing it meant another month off work. I took up my pen to write out his certificate and as I did so I thought to myself that I had learnt at least two lessons from this little episode. The first was that I would never again label anyone as a malingerer without first doing everything in my power to exclude real illness. And the second was that it appeared to be almost essential for the general practitioner to be an occasional visitor to the local pub.

5

"There, Mr. Smith. That should make you more comfortable," I said as I gave the old man an injection of chlorpromazine into the wasted muscles of his right buttock.

He made no reply, but his gnarled hands fingered the counterpane in a toxic, confused way and his eyes gave me only the faintest glimmer of recognition. His breathing was regular but rapid. Death couldn't be far away now and my patter had probably been entirely wasted because he was really too far gone to have taken in what I had said. But you could never be absolutely sure and I certainly felt easier in my own mind for making the effort to communicate.

I put the empty syringe back in my medical bag and straightened up as much as I could. At medical school my six feet hadn't made me tall as students went, but in this place I felt an absolute giant. The room was lit by the soft glow of an oil lamp and as I looked round I absorbed the scene with a sense of privilege for being there. Apart from the bed there was a simple wooden chair and a small wash-stand on top of which stood a large old fashioned jug and bowl with its small attendant soap dish. A clean towel had been laid beside the soap dish for me to use. From the wall above the bed a picture of Queen Victoria sternly surveyed the goings-on. If you discounted my medical bag on the lino covered floor and the chamber pot under the bed which had just made a pinging noise when I accidentally touched it with my right shoe, that was all the furniture and fittings the room contained. 'This was how it must have been in Dr. Long's day', I thought as I moved over to the wash-stand, poured some warm water from the jug into the bowl and proceeded to wash my hands. No electricity, no running water, no central heating, but in the flickering light of this tiny bare room the dying process seemed far more natural than in the sterile and impersonal surroundings of a hospital ward.

Herbert Smith had lived with his wife Alice in the same small thatched cottage for sixty years. For fifty of those years my patient had worked at Poplar Farm and the house was a tied cottage which had gone with his job. On his retirement his employer had behaved like many other good farmers and told Herbert that he and his wife could stay in their home for the rest of their days. So for the past ten years the ex-farmworker had been perfectly happy pottering about his garden and looking after his pig and a few hens. Despite their years of toil the Smiths had very few material possessions but up until recently they had been blessed with good health and they knew that that was far more important than all the riches in the world. They had six children and numerous grandchildren who visited them frequently, and when there weren't any visitors about there was always their cheeky little talking budgerigar to keep them amused.

But over the last few months the rural idyll had begun to crack at the seams. Herbert had started to complain of a poor appetite, loss of weight and difficulty in swallowing. When I had first been called to see him my clinical diagnosis had been cancer of the oesophagus, but I had been unable to confirm my diagnosis with X-rays because Herbert had steadfastly refused to go anywhere near the hospital. Nevertheless, his rapid deterioration in health had served only to underline my original suspicions and my visits to the cottage had become more and more frequent. I had come to know the Smiths very well indeed and their cheerful little kitchen with its chintz curtains, green painted cupboards and old fashioned fireplace with blackened kettle nearly always simmering on the hob had become almost as familiar to me as my own.

One day early in Herbert's illness I had called when the Smiths had been sitting down to their midday meal at their kitchen table. Herbert's helping of carefully cut up meat and vegetables was as tiny as I would have expected, but what really intrigued me was the sight of his ancient knife and fork. The implements had apparently belonged to his grandfather and had had a hundred and thirty years of continual daily use. Not surprisingly the two pronged fork was nearly worn down to the handle. The knife wasn't much better and Herbert's eldest son, Victor, had been pressing his father to some new cutlery in the hope, perhaps, that it would somehow aid the old man's digestion. But Herbert wouldn't hear of it. He reckoned his feeding tools would certainly see him out, and as it happened he had been right, for he must now be within hours of meeting his Maker.

I had been visiting at least once a day for the past week. The old man had developed a bronchopneumonia (which I didn't feel it my duty to try and treat) and I expected him to slip away quite quietly and painlessly.

I dried my hands on the towel, picked up my medical bag and prepared to leave.

"See you in the morning, Mr. Smith," I said, but there wasn't a flicker of response. Herbert's breathing had become stertorous and his eyes stared glassily at the ceiling. I groped my way down the steep and ill-lit narrow stairs to the kitchen.

Alice, her daughter Freda and sons Victor, Harry and John, with Victor's wife Mildred, were all crowded round the fire. The men got up as I walked in.

"How is he, Doctor?" asked Victor.

"Peaceful," I replied. "I think he will probably die before morning."

Alice bent over towards the fire from her chair and gave the coals a stir with the poker. The flurry of light from the revitalised flame shone on her brown wrinkled face as she did so and I saw that it was wet with tears.

"Tha's a rum un," she said. "He said he wor dyin' a month agew. But Oi'm glad yew didn't hev ter send him away, Doctor. He'd've hated that."

41

"Well, yes, I agree," I said. "It's all as he would have wished. By the way, if he does go in the night, perhaps you could get Mrs. Siggers from the village to lay him out?"

"That won't be necessary," said Freda. "Oi've done that job afore." She had too. A tough looking woman of nearly my own height, Freda had been a military policewoman during the war. Nothing frightened her, and she wasn't going to be cheated out of her chance to do her last bit for her dad.

"Oh good," I replied. "Well, I'll be along tomorrow morning whatever happens."

"Of course, Doctor," said Freda. "And thank yew for coming out after evenin' surgery."

"Not at all," I rejoined, a bit embarrassed by the gratitude. But it was typical. When you did nothing very much but watch the natural forces of nature work their way, people were grateful, whereas if you pulled off some modern medical miracle it was often hardly remarked upon.

Still, I had done my level best to be friend and comforter and I suppose that was worth something.

I said goodnight to my friends and went home to my supper in a humble and reflective mood.

Herbert did die in the early hours of the next morning and when I called round to the cottage after surgery the body had been neatly laid out with two old pennies in the eye sockets and a white scarf tied round the jaw and knotted on top of the head to stop the mouth falling open. I recognised the scarf as one which Herbert had often worn round his neck in happier circumstances.

I leant over the corpse and briefly listened for a heart beat with my stethoscope. There wasn't one, of course, so I pulled the sheet over the dead face and went downstairs again to comfort the family in the kitchen. They were all there, just as they had been the night before. I expect one or two of them had been away to their own houses and come back again, but it seemed as if they had been standing vigil continuously since my last visit.

"I really am sorry," I said. "But it's probably a blessing, isn't it? I wouldn't have wanted to see him going on much longer suffering as he was."

There was general agreement. Herbert had had nothing further to live for, and he was a lucky man to have died at home surrounded by those who knew and loved him.

"Tha's roight, Doctor," said Alice. "It had ter be. An' yew did yore best fer him, that yew did."

"Thank you very much, Mrs. Smith," I replied. "I'm sorry I couldn't do more. Will it be a burial, by the way?"

"Yes," said Victor. "We've told Sillett, the undertaker."

"Right," I said. "I'll leave a death certificate with Mr. Somerville in the dispensary if you could come up to the surgery late this afternoon to get it, please."

Victor said he would, and so, there being no further formalities for the time being, I excused myself and stepped out from the gloom of the cottage into the open air. The sun was shining, and although it was still only early March there was a definite smell of spring in the air. Out there in nature life was about to be renewed. Herbert might have gone but the daffodils in his garden would soon be in flower. The hens were clucking contentedly in their run, a blackbird was singing from the hedge, and as I walked down the garden path with the warm sun on my face I had a deep feeling of satisfaction which I had never had when I had lost a patient in hospital. This was the first time I had managed a death at home all by myself and I was buoyed up by a feeling of contentment. Even though the case had been hopeless from the start I had been of some definite use, and in the final analysis that's really why I had become a doctor, to be of use to people.

My pleasure was reinforced a few days later when I received a note through the post written in an untutored hand, which read —

Dear Dr. Slater

        Just a note to say thanks for tendin' Dad up during his last illness.

                V. Smith (son)

6

"Thass Fred Hillditch from Marsworth 'ere, Doctor."

"Yes, what's the trouble?" I snarled down the telephone receiver. It was nine o'clock on a Saturday evening and I had been on duty for the whole of one very frustrating day. It seemed that the telephone just hadn't stopped ringing and it so happened that I had, at that very minute, walked in after doing the last visit. My unfed stomach was grumbling for its dinner and my nerves were as taut as piano strings. I really wished I could have been as phlegmatic about life as Timothy Bacon who seemed to take days on call completely in his stride. It was a great source of irritation to me that on Monday mornings after Timothy had been on duty over the weekend I could never get him to admit that he had been busy, even though his call book carried very definite evidence that he had been. His standard reply when asked how the weekend had gone was, "Oh, not too bad. Didn't get any gardening done though."

Well, today I was quite ready to tell the world that I had been busy. Bloody busy; right up to my eyeballs busy. But Fred Hillditch didn't know that. Who was Fred Hillditch anyway? He talked as though I should know him, but I couldn't for the life of me remember who he was.

"There's a feller lyin' in the street just outside the post office 'ere," he continued, seeming not to notice my snarl. "'E's passed out an' 'e's got a card on 'im which says 'e's got diabetes. Could yew come, please?"

"Who is it?" I asked.

"The card says 'Alfred Fenner,' but Oi've never seen 'im afore." Neither had I — not to my knowledge anyway. And even though I had only been in Tunford for a few months I reckoned I must have met all the brittle diabetics by now.

"OK," I sighed. "Outside Marsworth post office you say? I'll be there in a few minutes."

I put the receiver down and stuck my head into the kitchen.

"Sorry dear," I said to Frances. "There's another urgent call to Marsworth."

"But your dinner's been ready for over an hour," protested my wife. "Can't it wait till you've eaten?"

"Fraid not," I replied. "It sounds like a hypoglycaemic coma. I'll be back as soon as I can."

As I tore out of the house and climbed into my car for what must have been the twentieth time that day, I consoled myself with the thought that this did at least sound like a genuine emergency. With any luck I might even have a chance to save a life, and after several months in general practice I knew how few and far between such opportunities were. Like many another doctor in the National Health Service my attitude to urgent calls had quickly become soured by very frequent false alarms. That isn't to say I didn't respond when they sent for me, but I had learnt that the words 'collapse' and 'haemorrhage' had a variety of interpretations. For instance, only that day I had had a frantic call to a tractor driver who was supposed to have 'collapsed' and turned his machine over on to himself. I had nearly broken my neck to get to him, only to discover that what had really happened was that he had stopped near a hedge to obey a call of nature and had sprained his ankle as he jumped out of his cab. The poor chap had wondered why I had arrived in such a lather and then torn him off a strip for not being more seriously injured.

But a diabetic in coma sounded genuine enough, and I covered the three miles to my destination as if I were driving in the Grand Prix. Marsworth was a little place roughly half the size of Tunford, and with its winding main street, ancient houses and higgledy piggledy moss-grown roofs it was, in its lack of symmetry, perhaps more attractive than its bigger sister. Naturally, most of the people who lived there didn't think of it or talk about it as being attractive. That was left to the occasional summer tourist, although I doubt if even a tourist would have been enraptured with the village on this particular evening, because the April air still had the nip of winter in it and darkness had fallen. The only sign of any activity was outside the post office where one of the Parish Council's four street lights illuminated the scene of an unusual drama. Unusual that is for Marsworth, because hardly anything ever happened in this little backwater where the sight of a pregnant cat would have been thought to be newsworthy. A group of about ten villagers was gathered round what looked like a bundle of old clothes lying on the pavement.

I parked my car and walked over to the gathering. I must say that I felt like running, but my old Professor of Physiology had always said it was unprofessional to run, and I think on the whole he was right. Style counts for a lot in a doctor, especially in an emergency. The bundle of clothing turned out not to be a bundle of clothing at all but an unconscious, thin faced little man with straggling grey hair. He wore an old army greatcoat and his fingers, I noticed, were long and delicate but heavily nicotine stained. From the top of his head to his badly worn boots he looked a tramp, and, perhaps not surprisingly if that is what he was, I had never seen him before.

"Here's that card Oi told yew about," said one of the onlookers. He was a podgy chap with flat hat and glasses whom I now recognised as Fred Hillditch. I had seen him in the surgery about three weeks before on account of piles, which accounted both for his familiarity with me and perhaps my own inability to put a face to the name over the telephone.

"Thanks very much," I said and took the card from Mr. Hillditch's outstretched hand.

It was a genuine card from the Angleton General's Diabetic Clinic made out in the name of Alfred Fenner. But otherwise it was blank. No insulin dosage. Nothing but the name.

"Where did you find this?" I asked.

"It was roight by 'im," said Fred.

In retrospect I should have been more suspicious, of course. It really was pushing coincidence too far for a diabetic to go into a coma underneath a street light, clutching his clinic card in his hand. But at the time I was far too busy thinking what to do next. And I was on stage too — a lot of eyes were watching me and I was very conscious of the fact.

I knelt down and made as quick and thorough an examination of the patient as I could in the circumstances. There were no obvious signs of injury, stroke or haemorrhage, although he seemed to be deeply unconscious. Taking into account the diabetic card, everything seemed to point to a hypoglycaemic coma, due almost certainly to the patient having had too much insulin and not enough food.

"He seems to be in coma all right," I announced to the crowd. "We should soon be able to fix that, but I think he will have to go to hospital anyway. Will you dial 999 for the ambulance please, Mr. Hillditch?"

"Certainly," said Fred, and he bustled off importantly to the telephone box twenty yards away to make the call.

I took a vial of Dextrose solution out of my bag, snapped off the top, and began to draw the viscous liquid into a 10 cc syringe. I had freed the patient's right arm from his greatcoat when I had taken his blood pressure, and now I partially reinflated the cuff of my sphygmomanometer so that it acted like a tourniquet and brought up the veins. There were several 'Ohs' and 'Ahs' from the audience as I selected a nice fat cord in the patient's forearm, thrust my needle into it, and drew some blood back into the syringe just to check that I had indeed entered a blood vessel. Then I released the air from the inflated arm cuff and began to inject the life-giving sugar solution into the patient's bloodstream. If this had been a film, the background music would have been working its way up to a crescendo as I emptied the syringe, because no sooner had I done so than Mr. Fenner slowly opened his eyes and said,

48

"Where am Oi?"

"In Marsworth," I replied. "I'm Dr. Slater. Don't worry. Just lie still."

The patient smiled weakly and I felt that the audience were almost on the point of giving me a clap, although I could sense that they thought it wouldn't be quite proper to do so — a bit like laughing in church.

Anyway, to continue my show of medical dedication at its best, I removed my coat, folded it and put it under his head. The man could well have had lice but I had decided to pull out all the stops over this one and besides, the old coat was well overdue for a trip to the cleaners.

Just then the ambulance arrived with its siren bleating and blue light flashing. It must have been cruising somewhere in the area when the radio message had gone out from Ambulance Control because the trip from Angleton usually took twenty minutes or so and it had been nothing like that since Fred Hillditch had made the call.

As soon as the vehicle stopped the two ambulancemen leapt out and ran the few yards to the spot where I was kneeling over my patient. Here were the U.S. marines coming to save the day again. Clear a path, their manner implied — the experts are here. But when they saw who the patient was, both of them suddenly lost that square-jawed look of the professional and their faces became quite rubbery and ordinary.

"Oh, it's him!" said the driver. "Can I have a word with you please, Doctor?"

"Of course," I said. "Fire away."

"Not here," he said. "Follow me."

I did so and we went round behind the ambulance away from the crowd. As soon as he thought we were out of hearing, he turned round.

"Don't you know Alf, Doctor?" he asked.

"No, I don't. Never seen him before."

"Well, I'm afraid you've been had. Diabetic coma was it?"

"Yes," I replied."

"Nothing of the sort. I'm afraid he's just an old scrounger after a free ride into Angleton. He does this to us from all over the county."

You could have knocked me down with a feather and I suppose my red face must have looked a very funny colour by the blue light of the ambulance.

"But he looked so genuine," I said, lamely.

"Well, never mind. You're not the first by any means," said the ambulanceman gruffly but kindly. "I'm surprised Dr. Bacon hadn't warned you about him. Anyway, we'll take him away this time, just to clean up the street. But please don't let him catch you again."

"No, of course not," I said.

I was flabbergasted. The hypoglycaemic coma had seemed to be absolutely genuine, and so had the response to my treatment. But then I recalled the paucity of information on the Diabetic Clinic card. And hadn't it been convenient that he had passed out holding the card just in the very spot in Marsworth where he couldn't help but be noticed? There was no doubt about it, Alf was a genuine one hundred per cent fake and I had been well and truly fooled.

Much subdued I followed the driver round to the other side of the ambulance and watched as he and his mate loaded the 'patient' onto a stretcher and into their vehicle.

The crowd began to disperse reluctantly as the ambulance drove quietly away with its blue light doused. I collected my things and climbed wearily into my car to drive back to Tunford and my long delayed evening meal. Suddenly I felt very tired and very, very hungry.

*

Three days later I received a curt little note from the Casualty Officer at the Angleton General. It told me what the ambulance driver had already divulged to me about Mr. Alfred Fenner, although perhaps not so politely. And as I screwed the letter up and tossed it in the wastepaper basket I thanked my lucky stars that my reputation in Marsworth remained unsullied.

The audience outside the post office that night would never know that they hadn't witnessed the dramatic saving of a life at all but the wool being pulled very firmly over a very green young doctor's eyes.

7

We hadn't lived in Tunford for many weeks before I found my way to the Angleton Rugby Club. Like an old war horse whose nostrils quiver at the smell of blood and sweat, I just couldn't resist the smell of stale beer and Wintergreen. When I had been a houseman in hospital it had been impossible for me to play my sport because I had had virtually no time off. But now in Timothy I had a boss who not only encouraged me to play Rugby but was actually prepared to stand in for me on a Saturday afternoon while I did so (I see now in retrospect that this wasn't perhaps all selflessness on his part because there is no doubt that I ran off a lot of steam on a Saturday afternoon and I am sure I was far better tempered the following week as a result).

From my viewpoint it was sometimes difficult to turn out on a cold winter's afternoon when I had been up half the night delivering a baby, but the healthy exercise and the camaraderie of the clubhouse after the match was worth it all, and when I had had a few pints of beer and sung a song or two the world would seem a much brighter place.

My sporting companions were mostly young farmers from all over the county, and I quickly came to enjoy their dry humour and respect their hard-headedness and native guile. At the numerous dances and social gatherings which took place, Frances met their wives and girlfriends and my better half and I were both grateful to have the Rugby Club to go to and mix with people who were round about our age and who weren't in any way connected with the practice in Tunford.

The Third Fifteen soon adapted to having a doctor in the side and Tony Mossman the captain positively welcomed me. Tony belonged to one of the long-established farming families in the area and was then aged about thirty five. He had been soldiering on in the front row of the scrum for many a long year, and like most front row men in an era when it was thought cissy to wear a mouth guard, he had lost his top front teeth more than a decade before. When he took his plate out before a game he looked quite fearsome, and one of his favourite tricks was to wrap his teeth up in a handkerchief and then like some knight of old present them to a girl spectator to keep safe in her handbag. It was surprising how many of the fair sex seemed to like the habit.

But that was typical of the man. He had generations of wily farming folk behind him who were used to making the most of their assets and driving a hard bargain. With such a captain the true value of having a doctor in the club was quickly realised. It wasn't, of course, to treat our own injured. Not likely! Confidence in my diagnostic skill had begun to evaporate the first time I had played for the team, when I had strapped up the fractured ankle of our fastest wing threequarter and told him to keep playing. True, we were losing eight—eleven at the time but that wasn't regarded as a mitigating circumstance when the poor chap subsequently had to have four weeks off work.

The very next week I had told a man with a dislocated shoulder to keep playing, arguing that he couldn't come to much harm if he didn't allow himself to be tackled. Tony hadn't been too impressed, and from that moment onwards my sole duty on the field was to flaunt my medical qualifications at the opposing side and send off as many of their players as I possibly could.

Every game of Rugby produces a few stoppages due to minor injuries and if one of the opposition went down with a bruised thigh, for example, members of our team quickly learned to give advice, which would go roughly as follows —

Our man, "Nasty looking haematoma, that."

Their man (seeds of doubt having been sown), "What's a haematoma?"

Our man, "Don't worry, we've got a doctor here. Just lie still."

The rest was easy. I would make a brief examination and invariably send the patient off the field. For quite apart from the tactical advantage thus gained, I could justify my actions to anybody by pointing out, that with my record of misdiagnosing sports injuries, this was probably far and away the safest thing to do anyway.

The medical sending-off ploy had been working satisfactorily to our advantage for several weeks when, at last, we came upon a team whose captain was at least Tony's equal.

We were playing away at the time, against a Norfolk side whose Rugby pitch was practically on the seashore. The wind howled in from the North Sea and we shivered with cold as we changed in an ancient stable at the back of a pub just across the road. Both First and Third teams were in attendance and since there was only one pitch, those of us in the less exalted team had to put track suits on over our Rugby strips and watch our betters play their game before we could even start our contest. As well as cheering and jumping up and down to keep warm we did our best to keep play going by shooing off a small herd of bullocks which periodically wandered on to the pitch. The animals seemed deeply resentful of their grazing being interrupted by a lot of peculiarly dressed human beings who had nothing better to do than chase an oval ball about. But, to us, the bullocks were at least a distraction from the game which was proving absolutely disastrous — if you were an Angleton supporter. Our First team took a real hammering, and the sight of such a debacle was no good at all for those of us who were just about to play. It was like having a preview of your own funeral.

I don't think our players were at all sorry to hear the final whistle, and as they were clapped off the field and we nervously prepared to go on, Tony was approached by the opposing Third Fifteen captain, who was a shifty looking little man of about forty with no teeth, a bald head and peculiarly close set eyes.

"We've only got ten men," he said unctuously, but in a voice we could all hear. "All right if we fill the gaps with some First Fifteen players? They say they don't mind playing again."

All Tony's instinct and experience told him that he shouldn't say yes, but he couldn't see any sportsmanlike way of refusing. You couldn't really expect a team to play against you with a deficit of five men. One man down would be fair game, but not five. He no doubt consoled himself with the thought that their First team would probably be worn out by now when he grudgingly said, "OK. But I think it's a bit much when you can't raise a full side on your home ground."

"I agree, old chap," said the other captain, "But they've all started drilling round about here." Drilling was one of the standard excuses for not being able to play Rugby in East Anglia, the others being potato lifting or sugar-beeting. Delivering babies just wouldn't have been acceptable. "Anyway, thanks a lot. You're a sport," continued the other captain.

Tony grunted a reply and we all moved onto the pitch to start the game. From our point of view we might as well not have played. It was a disaster. Even the bullocks seemed to lose interest in what we were doing. Right from the kick off the opposition out-scrummed us, out-jumped us and out-ran us. From my position in the second row of the scrum, I wore my heart out cornerflagging in defence time and time again. But their threequarters seemed to be incredibly fast and if you did get a tackle in there always seemed to be a man over to accept a pass and scurry for the line. At half time we were twenty three—nil down and we got a real telling off from Tony as we gathered around him in a panting dishevelled circle.

"For Christ's sake, keep the ball tight!" exhorted our captain, in between gummy sucks at his orange. "And if we get half a chance, use the doctor ploy. OK, Doc?"

I nodded assent. To hell with medical ethics and the prostitution of my profession. This was war.

Too soon the game restarted, and despite the pep talk the

play followed exactly the same pattern. We worked and worked, but they ran in try after try. Then suddenly it happened. One of their men failed to get up after a loose scrummage. The game stopped and the referee went to look at him as he writhed on the floor.

"We've got a doctor here," said Tony helpfully.

The referee looked relieved and I stepped forwards to look at the prostrate form. As far as I could discover the poor chap had merely been winded and was recovering rapidly. But I did my stuff.

"I think he may have a fractured rib," I said. "He'll have to go off."

"I'll be all right," protested the player breathlessly as he painfully got to his feet and assumed the hands on knees stance of the clapped out rugby player.

"Better do as the doc says," said the referee, and two of the injured man's team mates helped him to the touchline without any more argument. Somebody put an overcoat over his shoulders and he crouched there glowering at us as we took up our positions on the field again. The referee was just raising his whistle to his mouth to restart the game when John Copsey, our full back, let out a howl of anguish. We turned round, thinking that he had been stricken by the cramp or perhaps even a coronary thrombosis.

"What's the matter?" several of us asked in unison.

"The buggers," he yelled. "They've been playing with sixteen men." It was true. Despite having just had a player sent off, the opposition still had fifteen men on the field. And their shifty looking captain was looking shiftier than ever.

8

"You take as much as you like," said Timothy. "There's far more than I need. But for goodness sake try to keep it tidy, won't you, or else Mr. Baldry will be after both of us."

"Well, you know what I am about tidiness," I replied, "but I'll do my best. Thanks anyway."

It was another morning coffee session and I had been having a little moan about the lack of space for horticulture in the pocket sized garden at the rear of the surgery cottage. From there the conversation had led on to this offer for me to use some of my colleague's land.

Like nearly everything else to do with the practice, Timothy's garden was more or less as it had been when Dr. Long had laid it out fifty years before. It was an absolutely superb oasis of peace in which the doctor could escape from his patients for a while. The three acres contained a tennis court, a small orchard, rose beds, lawns and a fair sized kitchen garden which was noted for its mature and productive asparagus bed. A ten foot wall, complete with fig and peach trees on its southern face, hid a large part of the sanctuary from Tunford street, while the privacy of the rest was achieved with trees, some well placed shrubberies and a tall yew hedge. I had fallen in love with the garden the first time I had seen it and I was delighted that Timothy had seen fit to let me stake a claim in the vegetable plot.

But I might have been a little less delighted if I had realised quite what I was in for from Timothy's gardener, the afore-mentioned Mr. Baldry. For Mr. Baldry was to leave me in no doubt at all about who was to be boss in that garden. Small, wizened and stooped from fifty years following the plough, the old boy had only taken up part-time gardening when he had retired from farmwork. He was still as strong as a horse and extremely proud of the fact that, until my arrival on the scene, he had managed the garden on his own, with perhaps some slight help from Timothy, whereas in Dr. Long's day there had always been a full-time gardener and two boys employed to do the job. And now Mr. Baldry set out to cast himself as that long dead head gardener with Timothy and me as the two incompetent boys.

I must admit that he did allow us some status where the practice of medicine was concerned and would sometimes even cadge a bottle of medicine for a cough, or some pills for his arthritis. But in matters relating to the soil his word had to be law and I soon found it very unnerving to have him standing over me while I was working. I don't know if he had a positive plan for breaking my morale but, if he did, it was magnificent in its simplicity. A sort of water dripping on stone nagging which, within weeks, had me gritting my teeth as soon as I heard the old man's voice.

If I were planting a row of peas he would lean on his spade watching; patiently waiting until I had covered the seeds and was just firming the bed down with the heel of my rake, then he would be sure to say, "You've planted 'em too thick."

With the next row I would take his advice and plant fewer seeds, only to be rewarded with, "Toime the moice 've 'ad theirs, there'll be none left for 'un." I just couldn't win.

Timothy, who was terrified of his employee, had to content himself with mowing the lawns on a motor mower. He wasn't allowed anywhere near the kitchen garden except to admire it, because, on pain of the gardener's resignation, the really skilled job of tending the vegetables for the Bacon household had to be left strictly to Mr. Baldry, who also insisted that he should be the one to judge when the crops were ready for use. The trouble with this policy was that the gardener liked to grow things to their maximum size to demonstrate his prowess, and huge marrows or very stringy runner beans would be dumped at the kitchen door for Mrs. Yallop with a proud, "There's yer marrer," or "There's yer beans then." They were certainly prize looking specimens as far as size went, but not half so succulent to eat as younger and smaller vegetables would have been. I remembered the mouth watering stuff which my Uncle Jack had grown on his allotment back home. His motto had been 'Pick it young' and now that I was starting out as a gardener myself I determined to follow the same creed, despite Mr. Baldry.

But although the old boy resented my presence in the garden at first, as time went on a working relationship developed and we began to have quite long chats as we rested from our respective labours.

Like many ex-farmworkers of his generation Mr. Baldry was a bit of a long playing record when it came to talking about how tough it was in the old days. And I have no doubt that the work was very hard and the wages very low. But he had been a horseman, and when he spoke with affection about the Suffolk punches who had been his working companions for so many years, you had the feeling that there had been compensations in it all.

He had lived in Tunford for nearly all his life, the only break being during the 1914—18 War, when he had served in France as a machine gunner. When he talked about that terrible conflict he did so with a certain pride in his voice and a look of faraway horror in his eyes. But being Mr. Baldry, the awful experience he liked to yarn about most hadn't taken place on the Somme or the Ridge at Passchendaele, but in Tunford village hall where he had his medical examination before he had been recruited. A lady doctor (yes, a lady doctor) had had the effrontery to tell him to drop his trousers and had then proceeded to feel his balls. It wasn't, he thought, the way to treat a man who had offered to give his all for King and Country, and for a time his confidence in himself had been severely shaken.

There was no doubt though, that the old man's self esteem had now fully returned and he felt that he should be complete master of the garden, Timothy and me.

It was a situation in which I felt uneasy. A certain amount of egalitarianism didn't go amiss with me, but somehow total domination by a paid employee just didn't seem right. It was all very well for Timothy Bacon. He had been brought up with a nanny and was used to that sort of thing, but I wasn't.

One fine day in April I had my first real chance to show the stuff of which I was made. I was busy hoeing weeds among my shallots. The blackbirds were singing, the sun was shining and I was really enjoying my half day off. I had had the garden to myself for about an hour, and for this I thanked Compost, the God of gardening, but then, out of the corner of my eye, I saw Mr. Baldry shambling up behind me. I continued working but steeled myself for the expected criticism. I wasn't disappointed for long.

"Ain't no good hoein' when it's goin' ter rain," he commented tersely, emphasising his point by spitting noisily on the ground as he finished the sentence.

"Oh hello, Mr. Baldry," I said, pretending to notice him for the first time. "I think you're wrong. The BBC forecast said it was going to be dry in the East."

Now we happened to live in the West of our county and to Mr. Baldry the county was the World and East Anglia the Universe. The West of England might as well have been Mars.

"That might have," he said. "But it said it was goin' ter be wet in the West."

"Correct," I replied as I momentarily stopped hoeing and turned to look him in the face. "Wet in the West and dry in the East. And we live in the East," I reminded him.

"No we bloody don't, bor," he said with a smirk of triumph on his face. "We live in the West."

There seemed little to be gained in arguing the point further. Despite Mr. Baldry, I continued my work and later I took a great deal of satisfaction from the fact that for once the forecasters were right. Although it rained cats and dogs in Devon and Somerset, in East Anglia we had a lovely dry day and my hoed up weeds withered and died as I had meant them to do.

9

"Oh dear. There goes the 'phone," said Mrs. Dawlish.

"All right. You cover yourself up and stay there. I'll answer it," I said, wondering why on earth Agnes always seemed to be out when I called. Agnes was Mrs. Dawlish's unmarried daughter and she lived with her elderly mother in a very large and inconvenient house on the outskirts of Kingtree. The place was two miles from Tunford as the crow flies, and I expect the twisting country roads made it half a mile or so longer. But familiarity with the drive didn't make it seem any shorter because I had travelled that way fruitlessly too many times for that. Mrs. Dawlish was one of our regular senders. She suffered from arthritis, occasional bouts of bronchitis and very frequent quarrels with her daughter. From our point of view it was the rows which were the worst of her afflictions, because they invariably made her arthritis worse and a message would go out for the doctor to visit. But this morning, unusually, we didn't seem to be in the aftermath of a row. I had arrived to find the old lady fully clothed downstairs, but complaining of breathlessness and a productive cough. I hadn't fancied trying to fight my way through her corsets in the kitchen, so I had sent her upstairs to get undressed and into bed before I had examined her. It had all taken quite a long time, of course, and I wished Agnes had had the sense to keep her mother abed and wait in until I had called. It was typical though. I expect she thought her time was too valuable for that, even though she was probably only at some coffee morning. I thought it would be ironic if it was in aid of 'Help the Aged'.

I went downstairs. The telephone stood on a highly polished small oak table in the hall. I picked up the receiver.

"Kingtree 260," I said reading the number off from the small perspex covered disc in the centre of the dial.

"Thank goodness I've found you," said Frances on the other end of the line. "There's been an accident on the Tunford-Kingtree road near Wentis Farm. A Miss Purvis has fallen off her horse."

"Is she badly hurt?" I asked.

"They didn't say. But it sounds nasty. The horse has been injured too and they've sent for the vet."

"That's all I need on a busy morning," I groaned. "Anyway, thanks for doing your stuff, dear. I'll get along there as soon as I can."

I put the receiver down and hared up the stairs again. Miss Purvis was an independent lady in her fifties who rarely troubled the doctors professionally, but I knew who she was because I had often seen her plodding around the lanes on her elderly mare and I had asked Timothy about her. Her animal was so old it was a bit of a joke and it couldn't possibly have had the energy to throw her off. It must have caught its foot in a pothole or something. Or perhaps Miss Purvis had had a stroke?

"I'm afraid I've got to go straightaway, Mrs. Dawlish," I said as I burst back into the bedroom. "That was my wife on the 'phone. There's been an accident."

"Oh goodness me. I hope it's nothing serious," said Mrs. Dawlish.

"So do I," I replied, as I snapped my medical bag shut and picked it up from the bedside chair. "You're not too bad anyway. A bit of bronchitis, that's all. If you can send Agnes up to the surgery later, I'll get Mr. Somerville to put up some tablets and medicine for you. And I'll look in again at the end of the week."

Mrs. Dawlish didn't have much of a chance to make a reply, because I dashed out of her bedroom and left her lying there naked like some doll of which a child has suddenly tired and thrown down. In a trice I was down the stairs, through the front door and into the driving seat of my car. My haste was most impressive. But why, you may ask, was I behaving thus? Why was I acting like a Spitfire pilot scrambling after the Hun when my old professor had said it was unprofessional to run? Well, partly, of course, the reason was natural concern for the victim. But mostly, I'm afraid, it was jealousy. Frances had touched the red button by mentioning that the vet had been called as well.

All three of our local vets were young and thrusting. Their surgery set-up was very smart with new furniture, polished floors, gleaming instruments and attractive young receptionists. Our premises just didn't match up at all, and we were made very much aware of it because our patients took care to make comparisons as often as they could. The vets' recent acquisition of a radio telephone system had been a further blow to our prestige and we had become sick to death of being chided with stories of how when they called the vet he was usually turning in the farm gate ten minutes later whereas when the doctor was wanted it usually took him half the day to get there. Timothy and I had considered buying radio telephones but we had decided that there were substantial disadvantages for us in making such a move. For a start it probably didn't do most of our problems any harm to wait for a while. The diagnosis of appendicitis, for instance, was often very difficult to make if you saw the patient too soon. And then there were the neurotics. We didn't want them to think that we operated some sort of dial-a-doc system. It was bad enough as it was. But I think the idea finally came to ground on the sand bank of cost. Radio telephones were expensive, and for us they were unlikely to be cost effective, because we differed from the vets in that we weren't competing with anyone for customers. We were in the happy position of having a virtual monopoly in our practice area, and nobody was going to telephone two or three lots of doctors and then award the business to the practice which responded best, as sometimes happened in the veterinary trade. You could say that that was a bad thing for the consumer, and justly demonstrated how the National Health Service had stifled the healthy competition of free enterprise. But we weren't the 'consumers' and anyway we were glad we were able to have an easy relationship with the neighbouring practices in Angleton and elsewhere. And on the whole I think the patients benefited more from this friendly co-operation than they would have done if we had all behaved like a lot of medical buccaneers with our cutlasses always drawn.

So we bumbled on in our old fashioned ways and continued to leave a trail of telephone numbers and called back home whenever we had been out for more than an hour. The system worked, and it was very rare for real emergencies to occur without one of us being found pretty quickly. But the GPO telephone was old hat when you compared it to radios, with all their 'over and out, Roger, Willco, Charlie' gobblydegook, and we had to admit that the vets definitely had the advantage over us when it came to appearing to be modern. But now Providence had sent me this golden opportunity to show those jumped-up horse doctors that our primitive communications were just as effective as their over-expensive contrivances. Thanks to Frances I had received the message almost immediately, and all I had to do was get there first.

Miss Purvis's accident had taken place only half a mile from Mrs. Dawlish's house and I was there before you could say veterinary surgeon.

I risked my neck for nothing though, because, would you believe it, the opposition was already there. I don't know how he had done it, but Duncan McIver, the youngest and best looking of the veterinary group was obviously well established at the scene of the accident. It looked as though he had been there for several minutes, and what's more he was being given the pop star treatment by a group of horsey young ladies as he bent over Miss Purvis's ancient nag which lay quivering by the roadside.

I turned off the engine, got out of my car, bag in hand and walked over to the group (it was unprofessional to run).

"Hello, Duncan," I said. "Where's Miss Purvis?"

"Oh she's back there," he indicated with a nod of his head. His hands were busy drawing up a huge syringeful of God-knows-what which he was obviously meaning to inject into the horse. The syringe was about the same size as the ones we use for washing out ears, but I didn't think even the vet would be doing anything so crazy as syringing a horse's ears at the road-side. I followed the direction of the nod. Miss Purvis was sitting in the hedgeback thirty yards away clutching her ankle. She looked a forlorn figure. I hadn't noticed her before because naturally my attention had been taken by the vet's group and I had expected to see her somewhere in amongst that melee.

"I see," I said, and moved towards my patient. There was a concerted gasp of awe and admiration from Duncan's fan club as he stuck his needle into the horse's flank and started to give the injection. Whatever was in that syringe must have been good stuff because the animal began to stagger to its feet almost immediately. 'Psychological medicine,' I thought, but the fans were most impressed.

"What's the trouble?" I asked Miss Purvis as I reached her.

"I think I've fractured my ankle, Doctor," she replied. "Is the horse all right?"

"Seems to be," I replied. "Are you in much pain?"

"Not when I keep still. I'm so glad it was Mr. McIver who came. He's marvellous with horses," she said.

"Yes, so I hear," I replied, biting my lower lip. "Now let's have a look at your ankle."

She had already removed her riding boot and it didn't take more than a few seconds to confirm the lady's own diagnosis. She had quite a nasty fracture of her right tibia and fibula.

"You've no pain anywhere else?" I asked when I had told her the news about the ankle.

"No, I'm fine apart from that. Poor old Pippa. She just

seemed to stumble and I fell off her. I landed on my feet, but the right one buckled under me. Oh dear, I feel so silly. Can you do anything?"

"Not a lot, I'm afraid." I replied truthfully. "It's a hospital job. I'll send for the ambulance as soon as I can, but meanwhile you had better sit tight. Perhaps I can get one of these girls to stay with you."

She nodded, and I walked over to the vet's crowd again. Jenny Cunliffe was about the only one of the girls I knew well. I had sent her into hospital with appendicitis only a few days after I had arrived in Tunford, so she perhaps owed me a favour. I remembered that along with a lot of other teenagers she helped out at a riding school in Kingtree during the vacations. And that's where all the rest of the girls must have come from. The whole place must have emptied when they heard about the accident. Watching the handsome Mr. McIver at work would certainly be more exciting than mucking out. Even I would concede that.

"Miss Purvis has broken her leg," I said to the ex-case of appendicitis. "Can you stay with her, please, until the ambulance comes?"

Jenny's freckled face fell about half a mile. "Oh yes, I suppose so," she said, casting a glance at her hero, Duncan. Or was it the horse?

"Come on," I said. "The horse is fine. Look at her."

It was true. The horse was now well on its feet and Duncan was ready to lead it off down the road to Wentis Farm where it was stabled. He had a short shouted conversation with Miss Purvis and then started off at a brisk walk. The horse looked ready to break into a trot and I wondered again what had been in that injection. The camp followers tagged along like Hamelin rats in the wake of the Pied Piper and pretty soon there was nobody left but Jenny, myself and Miss Purvis.

There was no doubt that the vet had carried the day. Here I was, a poor little Napoleon after Waterloo — no victory, no glory, no army and only my wounded to clear up.

67

"Right," I said. "I'll be off to the 'phone box, then. The ambulance shouldn't be long."

The two of them nodded but they still had their eyes on Duncan's retreating back. The vet's car was still by the roadside and it did cross my mind that I could possibly have used his radio to contact the veterinary practice and ask them to send an ambulance. But somehow my pride wouldn't let me.

I climbed into my car, executed a neat little three point turn and drove slowly off towards Kingtree and the nearest telephone box. As I passed the vet and his admirers he gave me half a wave and a supercilious little smile which cut me to the quick. I suppose it was wrong of me to want the horse to bolt, but I ground my teeth and stepped on the accelerator pedal. My car shot away with a roar but the old mare never flinched. As Miss Purvis had said, Mr. McIver was marvellous with horses.

*

The morning passed without further incident. I telephoned the ambulance from Kingtree just as I had promised and in due course Miss Purvis was picked up and delivered to the hospital. She had about three months in plaster, and it was a good five months before I saw her back on horseback. But while my patient was still getting about with the aid of crutches I heard a story in the Three Tuns which gave me a great deal of satisfaction. According to Daisy Woodcock, not long after Miss Purvis's accident Duncan McIver had been called to see a sick dog belonging to an old boy called William Battle who was a patient of Timothy's. Old William had been a shepherd and he thought a lot of his dog. It had been marvellous company for him since his wife had died and when the animal became ill William was really very upset. Duncan, of course, knew how much the dog meant to the old shepherd and so he made every effort to save it, using all sorts of expensive antibiotics and visiting every day for a week. Perhaps not surprisingly with that sort of attention the dog pulled through and William was delighted. Duncan was very pleased too, although he had begun to worry just ever so slightly as to whether or not his bill would be paid. He was quite right to worry because William hadn't got a lot. In fact he was almost penniless, and the thought of the bill had troubled him too. But he had come up with a solution and when Duncan made his last visit to the dog he made his proposition.

"Mr. McIver," he said. "Oi'm very pleased wi' what yew done fer moi dawg but Oi don't know how Oi'm goin' ter pay yew. Would yew loike a cockerel, bor?"

Well, a cockerel was a cockerel, and as Duncan was well aware, at least it would be tax free and difficult to divide among his partners.

"Why — er, yes," said Duncan.

"Then go yew and fetch it. That's out the back there."

William's little thatched cottage had quite a sizeable back garden, with a long concrete path leading to the chicken hut and a run made of wire netting. Duncan did as he had been told, went out the back and followed his nose to the hut.

Mr. Battle had once kept two or three dozen hens, but now he was down to six hens and two cockerels. Duncan cast his professional eye over the cockerels and he noted that one was a prime looking bird with shiny feathers and a proud look to it as it strutted about the run. The other was hardly worth a glance. It was a flea bitten thing and it had half its feathers missing. Duncan opened the door of the cage and started to stalk the best looking bird. He was just about to make a grab for it when he was interrupted from behind. Old William had made slow work of shuffling up the path because of his arthritis, but he was here now, and apparently only just in time.

"No not that 'un," he said testily. "Do yew take the other. Oi'm keepin' that fer the doctor."

10

I don't know why it always embarrassed me so much but it did.
Daisy didn't seem to mind at all, but often when I called into
the Three Tuns early in the evening I found her having what she
called a strip down wash in the kitchen. And being Daisy,
provided that there was nobody else about she would usually
come out and serve me just as she was. That is in her pink slip
with soap behind her ears. I was used to looking at naked flesh
all day long but somehow the circumstances were so incongruous
that I would do my best not to give her more than a glance as I
paid for my beer. This evening was no different. I had started
into a conversation all right, but I was busy trying to look
anywhere but at the publican.

"Mendelssohn's Violin Concerto, eh bor?" said Daisy. "That'll
be three and sixpence for the beer and crisps."

"Yes," I replied. "Mendelssohn's Violin Concerto. Only the
Adagio mind you," and I handed over the money.

Daisy rubbed some of the soap out of her right ear with her
towel, and then to my very great surprise she began to whistle
the familiar piece of music as she walked back into the kitchen.

"Oi'll be there, moi lad," she shouted over her shoulder as
she started her ablutions again.

I sat down on one of the wooden benches in the bar and
sipped my beer as I waited for her to finish washing and dress.
I wished I had kept my mouth shut, because Daisy was the last
person I wanted there. But I had gone and told her and the only
thing I could hope for now was that she would forget.

"Did Oi ever tell yew Oi used ter walk out with a violinist?"
she said when she returned, respectably dressed now.

"No. What was he like?" I asked.

"A rotten bugger," replied Daisy, and then started a long

and involved story about this man of hers. I was quite pleased really because I thought it would take her mind off Mendelssohn's Violin Concerto. By the time I left the pub I knew quite a bit about Daisy's old romance and I prayed fervently that her memories of rotten violinists would keep her away from Tunford Village Fete. Because that's where I had agreed to perform the Adagio from Mendelssohn's Violin Concerto. I was not, let me hasten to explain, by any means a concert violinist and it was only under extreme pressure from Mrs. Griffiths, Tunford's leading music teacher and self-appointed impresario, that I had agreed to take part. I had played the fiddle since I was eight years old but there had been several gaps, sometimes of years and sometimes of months, in which I had been unable to find the time or the enthusiasm to practice. In an unguarded moment I had mentioned to Mrs. Griffiths that I was a violinist of sorts soon after we had moved to Tunford, and it hadn't been long before I had found myself playing second fiddle in a scratch orchestra which she got up to play Handel's Messiah in the church at Christmas. Now that wasn't too bad. When you had others to carry you through, the odd bum note or missed phrase didn't matter too much. But this latest venture of Mrs. Griffiths' was altogether a different matter. You see, she had had this, what seemed to her divine, inspiration that it would be a good idea to get a succession of 'noted' local musicians to play music in the church the whole of the afternoon on which the Village Fete was going to be held in the Rectory garden. On a fine day she thought that it would persuade a certain number of people to wander into the church and perhaps leave some money in the collection box, whilst on a wet day the music would really come into its own as an alternative attraction.

I had been terrified when she had first suggested that I should take part, but she had kept on cajoling me and flattering me until I had eventually caved in and agreed to do so. Her selling points had been that a full audience would be unlikely (given the average Tunford person's low musical tastes) and the whole thing was in aid of the church fabric fund, so how could I refuse?

What she didn't tell me was that as soon as I said yes she would go round the village telling all her friends that she had won the doctor over, and if they wanted a real treat they should be in the church on the day of the Fete to hear him make Yehudi Menuhin sound like a street busker.

I regretted my commitment as soon as I had made it, but I decided that I would have to make the best of a bad job. The abridged version of the Adagio which Mrs. Griffiths had found for me certainly wasn't beyond my competence when nobody was listening, but terrible things can happen to string players when they get nerves, and I was very worried that I would muff it all with the shakes in my bowing arm.

For the few weeks leading up to the fete I practised and practised. Frances got thoroughly fed up with me playing the tune over and over again and then agonising about fairly minor mistakes. The day before the fete my anxiety was at fever pitch and I thought about feigning illness. But then I thought better of it because everyone would know I had been chicken.

As usual the Rector had prayed for sunshine on the great day, and for once his prayers had been answered. He was delighted, and so was I, because I thought it was far less likely that people would want to go into the church if they could play hoop-la or eat cucumber sandwiches in the Rectory garden.

I didn't plan to go to the fete proper. I had a very light lunch (for which I had little appetite) and afterwards I got out my fiddle and played the piece through four more times. Naturally, I still made some small mistakes, but I thought I had it as good as I ever would, so I carefully tuned the instrument and put it away in its case.

Ten minutes before the time appointed for my execution I turned up at the church. As I walked through the graveyard I could hear the noise of a barrel-organ and lots of laughter and shouting coming from the Rectory garden. I couldn't see anything because of the Rector's laurel hedge, but it sounded as if the fete was going well. Inside the church, thank goodness, it was almost as peaceful as it was in the graveyard. Mrs. Griffiths was playing a gentle dirge on the organ and only three old ladies were listening to her.

They looked as if they had come inside just for the sit down. And who could blame them? It was nice and cool in the church and sitting listening to music was far less energetic than playing hoop-la. I smiled at them and I was rewarded with a brief, shy flash of three pairs of false teeth in return.

I walked down the aisle and put my violin case down on a front pew. Mrs. Griffiths gave me a nod from the organ and I unfolded my music stand and set it up in the centre of the aisle, just under the pulpit. The three old ladies watched me intently. Strange to say I wasn't very nervous. Playing to just three old ladies didn't seem to be too much of an ordeal at all.

I took my violin out of its case and gently plucked the strings to make sure it was still in tune. Then I tightened up the hair on the bow and got to work with the rosin. I think the psychiatrists would have called all this preparation 'useful displacement activity', and it certainly helped to keep me free of any great anxiety until I had finally finished and sat down on the front pew with my fiddle held gently under my arm. Then I began to sweat. I said a prayer and looked to the front, trying hard to concentrate on Mrs. Griffiths and the organ. But after a few minutes I began to hear slight creaking and shuffling noises behind me. I turned round and saw to my horror that the church was slowly filling up. All Mrs. Griffiths' middle class, middle-aged friends were rolling up to hear the doctor do his turn. 'Don't panic, Slater,' I tried to tell myself, but my mouth went dry and my knees began to knock nevertheless.

All this while Mrs. Griffiths had been working up to her finale, and as she came to her last chords she leant back on her organ stool and gave me a 'get up' sign with her left hand.

The organ music died away and I stood up and walked over to my music stand. Because we were in church there was no clapping for Mrs. Griffiths and no introduction for me (I didn't need one, anyway). My knees were like jelly and as I straightened out my music I could see to my horror that there was now an audience of thirty or forty people. And right up in the third row from the front was Daisy Woodcock. She must have just closed and she had that glassy eyed look on her face which we often saw on high days and holidays when the Three Tuns was full, and there were lots of people around to buy her drinks.

But I tried to pretend I hadn't seen her. I stuck my violin under my chin and took up my stance. My knees wobbled almost uncontrollably and my bowing arm behaved in exactly the same manner as I played the first note. The curse of the violinist had struck me. I had the shakes.

The note which I had meant to play was a smooth E natural with lots of tone in it, but what had come out was a flat and tremulous squeak which quickly lost itself among the ancient roof timbers of the church.

I gritted my teeth and tried to get a hold of myself. To a degree, I succeeded and the next few notes came a lot more easily. I was just beginning to settle down and really play myself into the piece when Daisy's voice piped up.

"Yew're holdin' yore bow wrong, dearie," she shouted.

I tried to ignore her, but beads of sweat broke out on my brow. I felt just like an English comedian on the stage of the Empire Theatre, Glasgow. Daisy started to la la the tune loudly, completely ignoring the shushing of the audience.

Then she butted in again.

"Oi tell yew. Yew're holdin' yore bow wrong, dearie," she repeated. There were a few little titters and I couldn't stand it any longer. My nerve snapped and I stopped playing. Suddenly all was quiet and my heels clicked audibly on the stone floor of the aisle as I stepped forwards towards my tormentor. Luckily she was sitting on the end of the pew and so I was able to put my mouth right up to her lug and whisper, "For Christ's sake shut your trap." I know it was blasphemy (and in church too) but it worked. Daisy clucked a bit, just like an old hen whose egg you have just pinched from under her on the nesting box. But she didn't peck, and after a while she settled her ruffled feathers down on the pew again and I had no further trouble.

Red faced, I went back to my playing position and started the Adagio from Mendelssohn's Violin Concerto all over again. Somehow, the venting off of steam seemed to have dispelled my nervousness. I attacked the piece with some gusto and played it through without any further hitches.

I think most of the audience were quite appreciative, although of course I can't speak for Daisy. But when the ordeal was over, and I gratefully staggered out into the sunshine, I resolved that I would never again expose myself in such a manner. I was obviously just not the stuff from which concert violinists are made.

And even now after several years if ever I sit dozing in front of a flickering fire on a winter's evening, listening to a gramophone record and imagining myself on the concert platform at the Albert Hall, my dreams are always traumatically interrupted by a glassy eyed old woman shouting, "Yew're holdin' yore bow wrong, dearie."

11

He had knocked on the door of the surgery flat and I had answered it. Before he opened his mouth I knew he was an American. With that close cropped head, those hornrimmed glasses and his checked shirt he could hardly be anything else.

"Are you the doctor?" he asked.

"Yes, I'm Dr. Slater," I replied.

"Thank goodness," said the American in his not unattractive drawl. "My son's cut his hand on a piece of glass and I think it needs a suture."

I looked beyond him into the street. A Volkswagen caravan-ette was parked at the kerbside, and in the back of the vehicle sat a very attractive blonde woman with a child on her knee. The child looked as though he had been crying. He was about six years old.

"OK," I said. "Bring him along. I'll open up the surgery."

This was the one advantage of living over the premises. When I was on duty it wasn't too difficult at all to deal with the minor casualties, and I enjoyed a bit of stitchery, even though it was Sunday afternoon.

I went round to the surgery door and unlocked it. Meanwhile the American slid back the rear door of the caravanette so that his wife and child could get out. I noted that the boy had a bloodstained handkerchief wrapped around his right hand. He carried the hand up in front of his chest for all to see.

"It's all right, Freddie," said the American to his son. "You'll soon be patched up."

They all followed me into the waiting room.

"You here on holiday?" I asked.

"Yes," replied the husband. "We've just had a month touring Great Britain. We thought we'd get home for the Fall. Our flight leaves Heathrow on Tuesday . . . Gee, isn't this cute. Just look at those beams, Elfreda."

"I'm afraid it must look a bit old fashioned to you," I said apologetically. "Anyway, come through to the consulting room."

"Don't apologise for it being old," said the American. "We just love your old English houses. I've never seen a doctor's office with so much atmosphere."

"You go with Freddie, John," said Elfreda. "I'll wait out here."

"Do by all means," I said.

"Elfreda can't stand blood," John explained. "Come on Freddie. Let's follow the doctor."

I must admit that Freddie was showing true grit. He didn't seem at all concerned. Or if he was worried he hid it well. His father appeared to be a lot more jumpy and I saw his face fall a mile when he saw the accoutrements in the consulting room.

"It's very primitive," I said breezily. "But don't worry, things don't seem to get infected very often. Can you climb on the couch, please, Freddie."

The boy did as he was told and I switched on the Anglepoise lamp to give me better light. The child lay back and was really very good indeed as I unwrapped the handkerchief from his hand. He had a nasty one inch long laceration over the dorsum of his right first metacarpal bone which would require three or four stitches. Luckily there didn't seem to be any tendon injury.

"You're right," I said to the father. "That will need some stitches. Is he covered for Tetanus?"

"I guess so," said John. "He had a booster last year."

I got Freddie to hold his hand over an enamel bowl to catch the drips of blood. That bowl must have been in the surgery since Dr. Long's day because it was very old and chipped. I used it often, but now that the Americans were here I felt very conscious of how tatty it looked. I switched on the steriliser. In no time at all it was bubbling away and I plunged a needleholder, a pair of dissecting forceps, scissors, Spencer Wells forceps and a kidney dish into the boiling water and closed the lid down again. While I was waiting for the instruments to be sterilised I went over to the sink in the corner to wash my hands. As I did this I said, "What a rotten bit of luck. Are you staying around here?"

"Oh yes. We thought we would finish off our tour by having a few days in Marsworth with my wife's aunt and uncle, Mr. and Mrs. Beauchamp. I believe you're their doctor?" replied John.

"That's right," I said. "I never knew they had relatives in America."

"Yes indeed. My wife's mother came to the States just before the War."

"And what do you do back home?" I asked, hoping that he wasn't a bacteriologist or a public health inspector, because if he had been, when he got home he would have been able to dine out for months on the descriptions he would be able to give his American buddies on the conditions in the Tunford Surgery.

"I'm a lawyer," he said.

"Really. How interesting," I replied. 'God,' I thought. 'That's worse. These American lawyers are mustard on medical malpractice.' But I tried very hard to maintain the British stiff upper lip.

"Well, the instruments should be ready now," I said. I opened up the steriliser and took out the kidney dish with the large pair of Cheatle's forceps we had for the purpose. Then I fished out all the instruments and put them in the kidney dish on top of our ancient glass topped trolley. We didn't have any sterile towels or anything fancy like that, so everything had to be done from the dish. The one saving grace, however, was that we did have pre-sterilised foil wrapped packs, each containing a length of suture material and an attached curved needle. I opened one of these now, and without touching the contents, I dropped them into the kidney dish too.

"Won't be long now," I said as I went over to the sink to give my hands another wash. I had long since decided that it was impossible to achieve anything like surgical sterility in a place like ours, but I believed in cleanliness nevertheless.

When I had shaken my hands as dry as I could I went over to the child and started to clean his wound with some cotton wool soaked in cetavlon. I had poured the cetavlon onto the cotton wool straight from the bottle without diluting it and it was perhaps a bit too concentrated. The boy winced slightly.

"Gosh, that's a nasty cut," I said. "You did it on some glass, eh?"

"Yes," said Freddie. "It was a milk bottle."

"He was trying to help out by carrying the milk into the house," said his father. "He smashed one of the bottles but instead of leaving it and fetching my wife he thought he would be helpful and pick up the pieces. In fact he nearly got away with it, but he cut himself as he was putting a jagged bit of glass in the trash can."

"I see," I said. "That's what you get for being a hero. Well, I'm going to freeze the cut so you don't feel me stitching it up. You'll feel some little pricks in the side of the wound but nothing else, I hope. If you do have any pain you have my full permission to shout at me."

I drew up some one per cent Xylocaine into a ten cc plastic syringe and infiltrated the edges of the wound as gently as I could. The boy hardly made a murmur. I waited for a couple of minutes to allow the anaesthetic to work and then I began to insert the stitches. The young American was obviously not having any pain because he made no fuss at all as I passed the needle through both edges of his wound, tied the knot and cut the ends. He watched me with mute submission, mightily impressed that I could do all that to him without it hurting.

His father was obviously impressed too.

"Gee Freddie, I wish Uncle Elmer could see this," he said.

"Why's that," I asked.

"Freddie's Uncle Elmer is a hand surgeon in Baltimore," replied the American proudly.

Suddenly the needle holder in my right hand began to shake about quite uncontrollably and I found the next suture incredibly difficult to insert.

12

"Ah, there you are, Doctor. Glad you could come," said Bill Butters with a welcoming smile on his face.

It was eight thirty on a cold frosty morning and I had just driven the couple of miles to World's End Farm with Frances' valedictory speech ringing in my ears. My wife was a member of the Royal Society for the Protection of Birds and she didn't approve of pheasant shooting at all. I respected her views, of course, but I was born of a long line of poachers and somehow I think a bit of the killer instinct must have rubbed off on me. Back home, my uncle Tom had kept a whole street fed with his snares and gun during the depression in the cotton industry in the thirties and I had been brought up to think of him as something of a folk hero. Bill Butters would probably have given me the bum's rush if he had known about uncle Tom, but thankfully he didn't, and he had invited me to his shoot because he was a decent chap and wanted to reward me for services rendered.

The rolling countryside within our practice area contained shooting land as good as any in England. Rich businessmen from London paid hundreds of pounds a year just for the privilege of having a gun in one of the local shoots, and the chance of having a day's sport for free wasn't to be sneezed at.

The Butters children had recently had a spate of minor illnesses and I had been a fairly frequent visitor to the farm for a month or two. Bill and his wife Mary had three pretty little daughters. A lot of people thought it was a disaster for the Butters, not having a son, when World's End Farm had been passed from father to son for generations, but the family seemed to be a happy one nevertheless. Bill certainly looked full of cheer this morning anyway.

"Well it was touch and go whether or not I would be able to join you, but here I am," I said.

"Good man," said Bill. "And now I would like you to meet everyone."

The other members of the shooting party were standing at the door of the barn. Out of the six 'guns' I already knew five. I had been in practice only a year now, but that year hadn't been an idle one. I knew a lot of people. The only person here whom I hadn't met before was a middle-aged farmer from the other side of Angleton who was introduced as Dick Bradley.

"Nice to meet you, Mr. Bradley," I said as we shook hands. I also nodded and said hello to the five beaters who stood slightly apart from the 'guns' in their own little group. They were patients of the practice to a man. The whole party was well wrapped up against the cold and our breath puffed out in little clouds as we spoke. The dogs snuffled round us wagging their tails and giving the occasional yelp. They were anxious to be about the day's business and I must say that I too felt it wasn't the weather for hanging about. I hoped the party hadn't been waiting for me for too long.

"Whatever have you got there — an ack ack gun?" asked Bill Butters. My gun was a five shot repeater which I had borrowed off a Rugby friend for the occasion. I had known that it would probably be regarded as unsporting by real shooting buffs, but I had counted on the farmers not minding too much. As a matter of fact I don't think they did, but the gun nevertheless marked me out as a real greenhorn.

"It's the only thing I could borrow," I said apologetically.

"That's all right. I was only pulling your leg," said Bill.

"Right lads. Are we ready?" he continued. "Doc — you jump in the front of the Land Rover with me. The others can get in the back. Now beaters, you know what to do. The first stand is at the end of Clay Hill Wood. You start from here, go up the road and then drive the birds through the wood on to the guns."

The beaters nodded their understanding, the shooting party clambered into the Land Rover and we set off. It was only half a mile from the farm to Clay Hill Wood but it was a very bumpy half a mile along rough cart tracks. At the Rugby Club we had a chap we nicknamed 'Gulliver' because he didn't travel too well. I thought of Gulliver as the waves of nausea began to strike me. Perhaps it was the very early breakfast, or the way I had hared around to do a couple of repeat visits before I had started out for World's End Farm (much to the surprise and irritation of the patients, may I say) but my stomach wasn't up to much that morning. Just as I was beginning to think that I should have to ask if I could get out and walk, Bill Butters stopped the Land Rover at the edge of the wood.

"Everybody out," he shouted.

Everybody did get out, and none more thankfully than me.

"Now Doc," said Bill, oblivious of my green face. "You place yourself there by the stream. And Dick, you stand thirty yards to the right of the doctor over there." He pointed with his left arm. His gun was in the crook of his other arm. "Everyone else fan out round the bottom of the wood."

I took up my station and loaded my borrowed gun. The others had either special little canvas bags or bandoleer cartridge belts to carry their ammunition, but I had mine in a small hiker's rucksack. It was another thing which marked me out as a novice, but it was quite practical because I had my lunch box in there too. I stood and waited impatiently.

In the distance I could hear the dogs barking and the beaters shouting as they slowly made their way towards us through the wood. My pulse quickened as they drew nearer. There was a crackling in the undergrowth quite close to us and we saw a labrador panting along with its tongue hanging out. Then suddenly there was a shrill cry of alarm and a frenzied whirr of wings as a cock pheasant got up. Dick Bradley's gun cracked once and the bird crashed onto the freshly ploughed ground near where I was standing.

83

"Well done," I shouted, again displaying how new I was to the game. You just didn't shout that kind of thing to an experienced shot like Dick Bradley.

Then, within a few seconds of each other, three pheasants got up close in my range. It was like one of those fairground games where you have to shoot ping pong balls off jets of water. One after the other I brought them down, and all without emptying the magazine of my gun. I whooped with delight and Bill Butters shouted, "Christ Almighty. Leave some for the rest of the season, won't you!"

But I could see he was grinning all over his handsome face. He was glad that I was turning out to be a reasonable shot.

Several more birds were brought down by the other guns (and several were missed too). But then it was over and we all unloaded before we congregated around the Land Rover again. The beaters and the dogs made short work of collecting up the dead pheasants.

"I thought you said your shooting was a bit rusty," said Bill, addressing me.

"Oh, it's the gun," I replied. "Didn't I tell you it's got a radar attachment."

Bill laughed. "OK lads," he said. "Back in the bus. It's the sugar beet field next. But I think Dead Eye Dick here can run behind, don't you?" He meant me and not the real Dick. There was a murmur of assent, and the idea certainly had its attractions, even to me. At least I couldn't get sick if I went on foot. But my pride wouldn't let me.

"Not likely," I said, making sure of my place as we bundled on board again. At the next two stands, my shooting wasn't half as good, but by the time we arrived at the King's Head in Marsworth at lunchtime, I was quite satisfied to have another two kills to my name.

Guns, beaters and dogs piled into the public bar. Most of the assembly had brought luncheon boxes with them and these were now opened. The King's Head was far more up-market than the Three Tuns. They even did bar lunches and I was surprised that they tolerated customers eating their own food on the premises. But no doubt the proprietors were satisfied with the profits they made from the sale of alcohol to shooting parties. Bill had already started these profits zooming upwards by ordering a huge round of drinks, and as I waited for my pint to appear I sat down at one of the tables and removed the rubber band from around my luncheon box. I thought it had felt pretty light and now I knew why. It was empty! Frances had been so busy sounding off at me about blood sports that she had forgotten to pack my sandwiches. At least that was the charitable view. The other was that she had done it on purpose. I took the charitable view, of course, but if punishment had been intended it could have been quite a nasty one if we hadn't been in the King's Head.

"Can I have scampi and chips, please?" I said to the landlord. "And perhaps half a bottle of wine?"

"Certainly sir," he said. "Here's the wine list."

"Good God. What a fellow," said Bill Butters jokingly. "I expect you'll win the sweep next."

"What's that?" I asked as I took my first sip of beer.

"Well, we usually have a bet on how many birds we'll shoot in a day. It's two and sixpence in the kitty and the nearest to the number wins. The last bloke we had as a guest on the shoot won the sweep. And I warn you, we never invited him again."

"I've no need to worry," I said. "All my luck's gone for today. How about eighty four?"

Bill pencilled the number against my name on a grubby bit of card which he had taken from his pocket. Then he entered everyone else's guess and collected the half crowns from us all.

My scampi and chips arrived, and I made great show about sending back for more tartar sauce. Then I ostentatiously put a napkin under my chin and set about scoffing the lot in front of the sandwich eaters. They enjoyed pulling my leg and I extracted the most from it too, especially in my praise of the wine, which deep down I thought was rather mediocre.

You would have thought that the food and booze would have impaired my shooting later that afternoon. But not a bit of it. I went from strength to strength. For most of the time I had a stand next to Dick Bradley and twice I 'wiped his eye'. The term was new to me, and in case it is to you I will explain that it has nothing to do with opthalmology. To 'wipe somebody's eye' on a pheasant shoot is to bring down a bird at which the other fellow has already had two shots and emptied his gun (that is if he doesn't have a five shot repeater, and he shouldn't).

Dick was far too much of a seasoned campaigner to mind because, like me, he was thoroughly enjoying the day out in the open air in good company. From a very frosty start the weather had now turned out bright and clear. It really was a pleasure to be away from the cares of the practice for a while. That was the real joy of shooting; not necessarily the killing. And if the farmers didn't have an interest in the sport, no doubt half the woods and copses would be grubbed out to make way for sugar beet. It didn't need much imagination to make you realise what a disastrous effect that would have on the local wildlife.

The day wore on and when the last drive had been completed we all assembled back in the huge barn at World's End Farm. The beaters laid out the day's bag on the concrete floor and Bill Butters started to count the birds methodically. They were really beautiful creatures and it did give me a twinge of sadness to see them lying there dead. Perhaps Frances had a point after all. But if you carried the argument against shooting to its ultimate you should be a vegetarian. And my wife certainly wasn't that. She enjoyed her share of animal protein just as much as I did.

The bag didn't look to be more than seventy pheasants so I was surprised when Bill reached eighty in his count. And then eighty one, eighty two and eighty three. "That seems to be it," he said, and I sighed with relief. After all the ribbing I had had in the pub I certainly didn't want to win.

But just at this moment Albert Bramley stepped forwards. Albert was a tall rangy farmworker who had been one of the beaters. He knew me well and had lent an interested ear to the conversation at lunchtime. As the count had progressed he had been shifting from one foot to the other and giving me crafty little winks. I had wondered why, but I now found out . . . With a flourish like a conjurer taking a rabbit from a hat, he produced another cock pheasant from behind his back and laid it on the floor.

"Eighty four! The doc wins," said Bill. "That's the end of you here, my lad," he said with a laugh. I collected my winnings and had to put up with a great deal of banter as I did so.

Still chuckling, we headed for the farmhouse in high spirits. Inside, a huge oak table in the kitchen was groaning with food. We took off our top coats, washed our hands and then sat down to the feast. Bill prided himself on being a beef producer, and it was one of his slaughtered animals which formed the basis of the feast. As we tucked into the delicious roast beef and Yorkshire pud we swapped yarns, laughed and talked as though we hadn't a care in the world. Mary Butters was a first-rate cook and her husband was an excellent host. He made sure that the meal was washed down with liberal quantities of wine and afterwards there was brandy and cigars. I refused the cigars, but accepted pretty well everything else that was put in front of me. After the brandy we moved from the kitchen into the sitting room, had more brandy and told more yarns. It really was a splendid evening, but like every other good thing it had to come to and end. At about ten o'clock I remembered my responsibilities and said I would have to be getting back to Tunford.

"Must you?" said Bill.

"Yes," I replied. "My pass expired about three hours ago."

"Well, it was nice to have you," said Bill. "Even if you did wipe old Dick's eye a time or two. You must come again."

"I'd love to," I said. "I really enjoyed myself."

I said goodbye to the others and Bill and I went out to the kitchen. He found my coat for me and helped me on with it. Mary was still clearing up after us.

"That was an absolutely splendid meal, Mrs. Butters," I said.

"Glad you enjoyed it," she replied, smiling.

"I put a brace of pheasants in your boot, by the way," said Bill.

"Really? That's very good of you," I said. "I'm sure they will go down very well with my better half." Inwardly I wasn't quite so sure about that, but only time would tell.

Bill made a move to show me to my car in the yard.

"No, don't come out," I said. "It's cold outside. You've got your light on out there. I can find my way."

Bill reluctantly agreed.

I staggered out of the house and at my insistence my host closed the door behind me. The outside light illuminated the side of the house and the path leading to the back door quite well, but out beyond its range where my car stood there was inky blackness. I gingerly felt my way across the yard. There had been quite a hard frost already and underfoot the ground was slippery. The revellers inside would find this out later, but for the moment they didn't care. I heard a fresh burst of raucous laughter and then a male voice began to sing a song.

I found my car, identifying it by touch more than anything. The windscreen was frosted and I cleared it as best I could with my handkerchief. The rear window was iced up too, but the heater would have to deal with that when I got going. I got in, started up quite easily and then switched the headlights on. I revved the engine for a minute or so to warm it. Because the rear window was nearly opaque I couldn't see a thing behind me, but I knew I would have to back out and turn in order to reach the main driveway. I selected reverse gear and let out the clutch. The car jerked backwards and then after a few yards came to a forcible halt with a terrible scraping noise of metal on metal.

The engine stalled and I applied the handbrake. With a sense of foreboding I fumbled for my torch in the glove compartment and then got out to see what had happened. It wasn't a pretty sight. Although my car had suffered slightly, what was more important there was a large dent and a three foot long scratch down one side of Dick Bradley's brand new estate car.

The singing in the farmhouse had suddenly stopped and everyone poured out into the yard to see what had happened. It didn't take them long to find out.

"I'm most terribly sorry," I said to Dick as he glumly surveyed the damage by the light of Bill Butters's flashlight.

'Well, what's done is done," he said, with what I thought was great restraint. "At least I can still drive it. You had better go home now and give me a ring in the morning about the insurance."

"Of course," I said, consumed with guilt. "I really am sorry. I don't know how I could have been so stupid."

It was obvious everyone else thought the same. The spell had been broken and a perfect day spoiled. In a very dispirited state I apologised again, and yet again. But after a while I realised that apologies weren't going to undo the damage done, so I bade them all goodnight and climbed back into my car.

You can be sure that I drove home very carefully, and as I did so I ruefully reviewed the day's errors. I had taken an ack ack gun to a pheasant shoot, won the sweep, wiped Dick Bradley's eye and wrecked his car. 'Well, that's it, Slater,' I concluded. 'That's the last time Bill Butters will ask you to a shoot.'

*

But I was wrong. To my surprise and delight, towards the end of the season Bill rang me again and invited me to a cock shoot. A cock shoot, may I explain, is one in which they leave the potentially breeding hen birds for next season and just slaughter most of the useless males. If you are male yourself it makes you feel humble. You realise which of the sexes is really important. This time I went to another friend and borrowed a proper double-barrelled gun for the occasion. And I resolved that when the opportunity came I would guess such a ridiculous number that I would stand no chance of winning the sweep.

Once again we were blessed with a dry day. Almost the same lot of sportsmen turned up and I was glad to see that Dick Bradley's car had been repaired and he seemed to have forgiven me. But I didn't chance my luck too far and I was extremely careful not to 'wipe his eye'. In the King's Head at lunchtime I guessed what I thought was a very low number in the sweep. I thought the shooting had been going quite well (certainly my own had). But when it came to the count up in the barn that evening I found to my horror that I had won my bet again. The total was very low and my estimate had been the nearest. Everyone except me thought it was terribly amusing.

"Are you coming in for a meal again, Doc?" said Bill.

"Yes, I would love to," I said. "But I'm a bit muddy. I would like to go home for a bath and change of clothes if you don't mind."

"Not at all. See you in about an hour then," said Bill.

I drove home to Tunford, had a hot bath, put on my Irish Thornproof suit and then used all the blarney it seemed to impart to me when I explained to Frances that I would only be out for an hour or two. I really felt on top of the world. With the exception of the sweep the day had gone well. But I had to keep things going that way. On no account must I disgrace myself in the way I had done with Dick Bradley's car. That meant drinking in moderation and being extremely careful. To make doubly sure that I didn't hit anybody else's car I decided that I would park my vehicle well away from the rest. There was certainly plenty of space.

It was pretty dark when I drove into the farmyard. My headlights illuminated a neat row of expensive looking vehicles drawn up near the barn. I went past them and came to rest right over on the opposite side of the yard. I carefully applied the handbrake and switched off the lights and the engine. But it was only when I opened the door and stepped out on to soft, yielding and well manured topsoil, that I realised I had done it again. I had parked right in the middle of Mary Butters's new rosebed!

13

Imagine that you are lying in bed next to your spouse. It is warm and comfortable and you have just dozed off in a state of post-coital bliss. Outside the wind is howling and it is very cold. But in here, in this beautifully cosy, voluptuous bed, it is like the womb. And then the 'phone goes. You wake up, knowing that after you have answered it, you will have to go out. It's a terrible moment and not made any better by the thought that every winter's night in every region of the kingdom, some doctor will be suffering a similar experience which he will have to do over and over again throughout his professional lifetime. It's neither romantic nor funny. You just never get used to it, and as you get older it only becomes worse.

But night calls are not easy when you are young either. It was only three weeks after my first shooting party at World's End Farm when, for the fifth time that month, the bedside telephone extension rang shrilly in my ear during what are now called 'unsocial hours'. I groped for the switch on the bedside lamp like a drunk looking for his key under the doormat. At last I found it. The alarm clock stood at half past midnight, and we had only been in bed for an hour. 'Why the hell can't they leave us alone.' I thought. I picked up the receiver and put an end at last to the nerve shattering noise.

"Dr. Slater," I said, crossly.

"Ivan Moss here," said a voice at the other end. "Can yew come an' see Reuben Scase. 'E's 'ad a fall and 'urt 'is shoulder."

I knew Reuben and his habits well. He was often in the surgery complaining of a bad back. The back might sometimes stop him working but it never stopped him getting to the pub.

"Had one too many, I suppose," I said.

"Well not exac'ly. But he was on 'is way hoom from the King's 'Ead."

"All right. I'll come," I said. "Where is he now?"

"Oh, we got 'im 'oom orl roight."

"OK," I said resignedly as I put the 'phone down.

Timothy and I had a policy about night calls. We didn't argue, we just went. Most of the requests for after hours visits were perfectly genuine, and the ones which didn't sound that way weren't worth fighting about because sometimes a call which sounded absolute rubbish would turn out to be very necessary, and it was altogether too risky to try to diagnose and treat over the telephone.

I lay there and groaned for a few moments. It took a lot of courage to throw my half of the bedclothes back and get up. But as I did so Frances woke with a start. I thought it was incredible the way she could sleep through the telephone ringing like that, but then I suppose I was just as capable of snoring through it all when our daughter cried and my wife had to get out of bed. We had different triggers, that's all. And mine was definitely set on a hair spring for the telephone. So much so that I would jump like a Pavlovian dog whenever any bell went off, even when I was off duty or on holiday.

"Where have you got to go to?" she asked sleepily.

"Marsworth," I replied as I pulled an old sweater over my pyjama top. "I won't be long."

"Oh," she said. "Be careful of the roads won't you . . ." But almost before she had finished her sentence she was asleep again. I really envied her. 'Why wasn't I born a woman?' I said to myself. But then I thought of having babies and changed my mind. Why wasn't I a civil servant with a nice sit-on-your-backside-and-hang-your-hat-on-a-pension, nine to five job? Why indeed. But the die was cast now. An old pair of slacks covered my pyjama trousers. They were pretty threadbare but nobody (especially Reuben Scase) was going to notice at that time of night. I sat on the edge of the bed to put on socks and my suede slip-on shoes. Marsworth was only three miles down the road and I reckoned that I would be back in bed before you could say knife. But my goodness it was cold. I blessed the chap who had invented car heaters. Before he came along the GP's lot was even less of a happy one than it was now. And before that it was ponies and traps. The mind boggled.

I had another envious glance at Frances as she lay there in bed and then I switched off the light and groped my way to the landing. We usually kept the landing light on because of Sally, our daughter, and so the landing and the stairs were easy to negotiate. In the hall I stopped to put on my overcoat. I say my overcoat, but in fact it really belonged to a Welsh miner who had come up to play Rugby against my teaching hospital just before I qualified. He had taken my overcoat back to the valleys as some sort of trophy, and left his checked monstrosity to be worn by a respectable GP. I never liked the look of it, and what's more I had soon found that it wasn't equal to keeping out the harsh easterly winds of East Anglia. Not for nothing did the locals say the wind in these parts didn't stop to go round you but went straight through you. But for the moment the coat was all I had that was reasonably clean, and when I had put it on I dug in the pockets for my gloves. And as I did so I cursed Welsh miners, Reuben Scase, the demon drink and even Ivan Moss, who had done a very neighbourly thing and telephoned the doctor to come and see his injured friend.

When I had put the cat out before going to bed it had been very cold and the air had been still. But now when I opened the door I found that there was quite a strong breeze blowing and there had been a light fall of snow. It amounted to little more than a skittering and it didn't seem much to worry about.

My Morris Minor was parked in the street in its usual place. I cleared the windscreen of snow with a few sweeps of my gloved hand, unlocked the door and got in. To my surprise the engine started first time and I switched the heater on to full blast. In no time at all I was driving out of the village towards Marsworth.

The snow became deeper as I left the built-up area. The hedge-rows on both sides of the road had been slashed to their roots in the Autumn and I have little doubt that this contributed to the drifting of the snow on the unprotected road. I have heard farmers argue until they are blue in the face that hedgerows actually cause drifts, but I cannot for the life of me see how this can be true. I think it's just another attempt to justify their desecration of the countryside.

Anyway, the drifting wasn't serious yet and I was able to drive along at more or less my normal speed. I travelled the Tunford-Marsworth road pretty well every day and I was confident that I knew every twist and turn like the back of my hand. But perhaps I was a little too confident, because just a mile outside Marsworth I rounded a corner and ran slap bang into a two foot snowdrift. The car engine laboured and then stalled. I started it again and tried to back, but the rear wheels spun round uselessly. I was completely stuck, and right in the middle of nowhere. I swore and swore again. Then I realised that sitting there cursing wouldn't get me free, and I couldn't sit there all night. Nor could I dig myself out because I hadn't got a shovel. The only thing to do was to go and get help. The nearest habitation was Finbow's farm half a mile back up the road to Tunford and that's where I would have to head for. I turned off the engine and the lights. Fortunately my torch was in its usual place in the glove com-partment and when I switched it on it worked. I stepped out of the car and shut the door. Out in the open the wind was really howling and it nearly cut me in half. In that moment I believed implicitly that the icy blasts which rake East Anglia in the winter do come straight from the Urals. Within half a minute the cold had penetrated my miner's coat, my threadbare sweater and my pyjamas. My hands, feet and every other appendage quickly began to feel numb, and I realised that if I didn't get a move on, in the very near future my sex life would be nothing but a pleasant memory.

I trudged off in the direction of Finbow's farm. In a few yards my suede shoes were full of snow and the bottoms of my trousers were plastered with it. When I had stepped out of the car there had been no snow falling from the sky; whatever there was flying about had merely been whipped up by the wind, but I hadn't been walking for more than a hundred yards before it started snowing heavily and my hair soon became matted with the stuff. I plodded on desperately. Modern man is so protected by his technology that he forgets what it is like to wrestle with nature. For the most part he sits in a car or an aeroplane and views the outside world from a carefully controlled environment. It is only when his machines break down that he sometimes begins to realise how tough it is out there. Now I was learning something of what it must have been like to be one of Napoleon's troups in the retreat from Moscow. But those poor devils had to march for miles and miles without any hope of help. All I had to do was make it to Finbow's farm, and even that seemed far enough. I don't think I would have survived the little emperor's retreat. And if I had I can tell you with the utmost certainty that it would have been a case of 'Not tonight Josephine' for the rest of my life.

After what seemed an age I came up level with the Finbow's dwelling and walked into the yard. The dog, chained up in his kennel near the barn, started barking long before I reached the back door. A light went on and the back door opened.

"What is it, Ben?" I heard old William Finbow say to the dog.

"It's me, Mr. Finbow," I said as I got nearer.

"Who's me?" asked William.

"Dr. Slater," I said, drawing nearer.

"Well, bless moi soul. Yew look frozen, bor. Come roight in."

I stepped into the kitchen. Mabel came through from another room in her dressing gown. Her grey-brown hair was tousled with sleep and she blinked at me myopically until she had wiped her glasses and put them on.

"Goodness me, Doctor," she said. "Yew do look a sight. What's happened?"

"My car got stuck in a snowdrift about half a mile up the road," I said.

"It's no noight ter be out," said William. "Where were yew headin' for?"

"Marsworth," I said. "Somebody's had an accident. I still need to get to him."

"Well don't yew worry about that," said William. "We'll soon hev yew out o' that drift with the tractor. Oi'll go and wake Frank."

Frank was the Finbow's twenty three year old son. He could obviously sleep a lot better than his parents. William went off to rouse him.

The kitchen was lovely and warm. Mabel took up a scuttle full of coke and shook some of it into the top of the Aga stove.

"Take your coat off and warm yourself over here," she said. "Oi'll get yew a towel ter dry your hair. And what about a cup of cocoa?"

"Yes please," I said. I took off my gloves and the Welsh miner's overcoat and laid them on a wooden kitchen chair in front of the stove. Then I gripped the towel-drying bar which ran along the front of the Aga and waited for my hands to warm up. At first the warmth was ecstatic, but then my fingers began to tingle painfully as the blood started to circulate normally again and I had to take my hands off the bar and give them a good shake until the tingling stopped.

Mabel handed me a towel and then filled the kettle.

"Take your shoes and socks off," she said. "Oi'll find yew some Wellingtons and some of Frank's long woollen stockings which I knitted him. They're just the job for this weather."

I looked down at my numb nether regions. A little pool of water was forming round my shoes, and I was reminded of the time when I was a very little boy and I had wet my trousers while I was standing in the dunce's corner at school. How I had been shouted at for that. It had obviously scarred my memory for life. This time the liquid was ordinary melted snow but I was very grateful for the fact that the Finbow's had a sensible tiled floor and no fancy carpets.

I sat down on a chair and slowly removed my sodden shoes and socks. My toes were blanched and bloodless. I dried my feet carefully and put the shoes and the socks in front of the Aga with the rest of my discarded apparel.

Mabel had popped out of the room for a moment or two but she soon returned with a huge ex-army greatcoat and two pairs of thick woollen stockings.

"Here yew are," she said.

I put on both pairs of stockings, one on top of the other, while she made the cocoa. She handed me the steaming mug and I was just about to take the first sip when Frank came into the room. He grinned when he saw me and I made to get up.

"Don't yew move," he said. 'Oi'll bring the tractor up to the back door." Frank wore a thick sweater which nearly stretched down to the knees of his corduroy trousers. They in turn were tucked into a pair of long woollen socks. Near the door he stopped briefly to put on a heavy parka and some Wellington boots and then he was gone. William had returned to the room at the same time as his son, but he stayed in the kitchen.

"Feel better now?" he asked.

"Yes thanks, Mr. Finbow," I said. In the background we heard the tractor splutter into life in the barn. Then there was a revving of the engine and a deep throated roar moving up to a crescendo as Frank brought the vehicle across the yard and up to the back door.

I gulped the cocoa down and then put on the Wellingtons which Mabel brought me from a pile of footwear in a cupboard near the sink. The rubber boots fitted quite well and I stood up and donned the greatcoat. Frank came into the room. He gave me only the faintest of smiles when he saw me standing there in my new gear.

"Ready then?" he said.

"Yes," I replied, and I followed him to the door. "I'll see you later," I said to his mum and dad just before I crossed the threshold. "But thank you very much indeed. You've saved my life."

They smiled and nodded.

"Tha's orl roight," said William. "Now be careful tergither won't yew."

"Course," said Frank, and in a second we were outside in the snow with the door shut behind us.

The wind seemed to have dropped slightly but it was still snowing. The tractor stood there with the headlights on and the engine throbbing away. It looked solid and dependable. Frank climbed into the cab and shouted at me to do the same. There was just about room for the two of us to sit on the seat if I crushed myself over to the left, which I did. Frank was then left more or less free to operate the controls normally. He put the machine into gear and we moved off. The powerful head-lights cut a wedge out of the darkness and the descending snowflakes might have looked pretty had they not spelled trouble for travellers. I made fists of my fingers to keep them warm and then stuck them deep in the pockets of the greatcoat. There was no heater and the only warmth came from the engine and our own bodies. Still, I was immeasurably better off than I had been when I was on foot. The tractor churned through the snow and in no time at all we came to the place where my car had come to grief. It was now nearly buried and there looked to be no hope of getting it out. But although the snow was deep on the side of the road where my car was, on the opposite side it was a lot shallower and it looked as if the tractor at least might be able to make it on to Marsworth. I still had my patient to see and no doubt Ivan Moss and Reuben were wondering where on earth I had got to.

"Can we get to Marsworth in the tractor, do you think?" I shouted to Frank over the noise of the engine.

"Oi reckon so," he replied.

"Well, lend us your shovel and I'll rescue my medical bag."

Frank had had the good sense to put a shovel in the back of the cab. I climbed out of the tractor and he handed me the tool. I struggled over to my car and after a few minutes hard shovelling I managed to open a rear door and remove my bag. I had had my back to the wind as I had worked but when I turned round to windward again the driven snow whipped into my face and really stung it. Fortunately it was quite easy to see what I was doing because of the tractor headlights and I lost no time in getting back to the cab with my precious bag and the even more precious shovel.

"Right. Let's go," I shouted as I climbed in.

Frank needed no encouragement to put his foot down. We really churned forwards and the snow spewed out from the front wheels like the spray from the bow of a destroyer. Just once or twice on our way to Marsworth we slowed up and nearly got stuck. But by a bit of judicious reversing and then going forwards again at top speed we managed to burst our way through the deeper drifts. Not once did we have to get out and use the shovel and I should think it was only about twenty minutes after we had left my abandoned car that we at last pulled up outside Reuben's cottage.

Ivan Moss heard us coming and came out of his neighbour's house with a torch in his hand.

"Thank goodness you've come, Doctor," he said as I climbed down from the tractor and followed him down the garden path. "Fancy bringin' yew out on a noight loike this. We got the ol' bugger inside now but 'e fell down agin' on the path 'ere. Cor, didn't 'e swear. Now mind the step as yew come in, won't yew."

I watched the step as I was told and followed Ivan into the cottage. Reuben was a bachelor in his fifties and he lived on his own. I don't think many men bother much about tidiness when they live without the benefit of a woman and Reuben was no exception. His mother had died six years before and little but the most rudimentary housework had been done since then. The place was littered with old newspapers and a fair collection of empty milk and beer bottles of uncertain vintage. The whole house reeked strongly of stale tobacco smoke and beer and on a greasy plate on the sitting room table there were the remnants of a fish and chip supper. Reuben lay on a dilapidated Victorian chaise longue next to the near-dead fire. Somebody had tried to rekindle the fire recently, possibly using the wrapping paper from the fish and chips, but the attempt hadn't been too successful as yet because only a faint spiral of smoke coiled its way up the chimney. The room was very cold.

"What happened?" I asked the patient.

"Oi think Oi've bruk me shoulder," he replied succinctly.

"Let's have a look then," I said.

"Orl roight," he said. "But be careful. It's bloody painful."

Somehow I managed to get him to sit up and then I carefully removed his mackintosh, jacket, pullover and shirt. The procedure was a lengthy one but worth it to me in the end because when I was able to examine his left shoulder properly I came to the conclusion that it probably wasn't fractured at all. He had an anterior dislocation of his shoulder joint. Of course under normal circumstances I would have sent him to hospital for an X-ray just to make sure there wasn't a complicating fracture. And if the X-ray showed no fracture but only the dislocation he would have it put back by an expert, probably under general anaesthesia. But the situation was far from normal. An ambulance certainly wouldn't be able to make it to Marsworth the way we had come, and given that fact I felt perfectly justified in having a go at reducing the dislocation myself.

"I think it's only dislocated," I said. "I may be able to get it back, if you will let me."

Reuben looked at me very dubiously.

"OK," he said. He realised he hadn't much choice.

"Lie back then," I said, and he painfully re-adopted the half reclining position on the chaise longue in which he had been before I had removed his upper clothes. His teeth began to chatter and he eyed me very strangely as I took off my right Wellington boot.

"Don't worry," I said. "I have to do that because I want to put my foot in your armpit." My words didn't seem to comfort him at all. And as a matter of fact I was fairly uneasy myself because I had never reduced a shoulder dislocation before. I had read how to do it, of course, but that was before Finals. The most modern method would have been Kocher's manoeuvre in which the surgeon applies traction to the flexed elbow, rotates the arm laterally, adducts the elbow and then rotates the arm medially. But I couldn't for the life of me remember all that. The only thing I could remember was a picture, which had been in one of my textbooks, of a nineteenth century sawbones reducing a shoulder by pulling on the arm and applying counter pressure with his foot in the patient's armpit. It had seemed a lot more impressive than Kocher's manoeuvre and I suppose that's why it had stuck in my mind.

Some of those nineteenth century surgeons were pretty slick operators, and their methods were often just as valid now as they were then, especially if you were trying to cope without anaesthesia as I was.

"How much beer did you have?" I asked the patient.

"About foive pints," replied Reuben.

That was some time ago now, of course, but the circulating alcohol should help to numb the pain a bit, I thought.

I tried to exude confidence.

"Good," I said. "You've given yourself the premedication. For the anaesthetic I'll give you a pain killing injection. It won't put you out but it should help you not to feel anything very much."

In my heart of hearts I wasn't so sure about that, but I took a hundred milligram vial of Pethidine out of my bag and gave it to him intravenously. I waited for a few minutes to allow it to work. Then I grasped Reuben's left wrist tightly, put my stockinged right foot in his left armpit and yanked the arm towards me as hard as I could. According to the book at this juncture my right foot should have felt the patient's displaced humeral head slip gratifyingly back into place with an onomatopoeic clunk. But there was no clunk.

"Chroist orlmoighty. Leggo," yelled Reuben at the top of his voice.

I did so. Despite the cold I was sweating. The shoulder was still dislocated and the doctor—patient relationship almost fractured.

"Sorry about that," I said. "I expect it's so difficult because it has been out so long. But it was worth a try. I usually have one go at reduction," I lied, "and if that fails I send the patient to hospital."

Reuben nodded and held his injured arm tenderly to his side. The Pethidine seemed to have had no effect whatsoever.

"If we get you dressed again do you think you could get to the tractor?" I asked.

"Have to, wun Oi?" replied Reuben.

He would obviously do anything rather than risk any more of my tender ministrations. "That's the plan then," I said. "We'll get to Tunford by tractor and perhaps the ambulance will meet us there. I shouldn't think they will have difficulty getting to Tunford along the main road. Dr. Bacon told me that the snow ploughs usually keep that clear at all costs."

Reuben nodded. Ivan Moss had watched my performance with considerable interest. If I had pulled off the orthopaedic manoeuvre there would have been a lot to tell the regulars in the King's Head. The fact that I had failed meant that there would probably be even more to relate. But his face betrayed nothing of his thoughts as I turned to him.

"Can I use your phone please, Mr. Moss?" I asked.

"Course yew can, Doctor," he said. "Here Oi'll show yew the way."

"Hang on," I said. "Let's help Reuben to dress first." We

did, and then Ivan showed me round to his cottage next door as he had promised. I telephoned the ambulance control in Angleton and told them my plan. "Could you meet us in Tunford in about an hour and a half please?" I said. They agreed and I then rang Frances to tell her what was happening. She was quite relieved to hear from me. In her sleep she must have noticed the cold in her back caused by my over long absence from the marital bed and she had woken up and started to worry. I outlined the story of events so far. "I'm fine now," I said, "thanks to the Finbows. Keep the bed warm. I should be home in an hour or two."

"Good," she said. "It's cold here without you."

I put the receiver down and left the cottage. All this time Frank had been patiently sitting outside in the tractor with the engine turning over. I figured that I would have to ask my driver to take Reuben up to Tunford first and then come back for me. But when I spoke to him Frank had other ideas. He reckoned that with a bit of luck we would all three of us be able to get in the cab. I bowed to his superior knowledge of these matters.

"Come and give us a lift then," I said, and Frank descended from his perch in the tractor and came into Reuben's cottage with Ivan and me. Slowly we eased the patient off his chaise longue, out of the cottage, up the path and into the tractor. It was a long and painful process but we succeeded. Since my attempt to manipulate his shoulder Reuben seemed to have developed a new will to live and this helped a lot. Frank put the injured man in the driving position and then squeezed himself into the cab in a half standing position to the patient's right. He suggested that I did the same on Reuben's left. Somehow I managed it, but for once in my life I wished I was something less than a Rugby forward. And I wished too that Reuben had been some cuddly blonde instead of a stubble faced old codger in a flat hat and dirty mackintosh.

Frank explained what to do. He would be ship's master and work the brake, gears, steering wheel and throttle while

I would be the cabin boy and operate the clutch whenever I was told to.

We waved goodbye to Ivan. Frank turned up the throttle and shouted to me to let out the clutch. I did so very gently and we moved slowly forwards, gradually picking up speed as we ploughed on.

Fortunately it had stopped snowing while I had been in Reuben's cottage. The tracks we had made on the outward journey were still just visible but they were rapidly being filled in by drifting snow. Nevertheless, they were a guide through the shallower parts of the drifts and we managed to follow them successfully without once getting stuck. We passed the place where my car was and it was almost invisible. I wondered how I was going to cope with my visits later that day without it. As it happened I needn't have worried one bit because I had about ten offers to loan me a variety of vehicles as soon as the news got out. None of them were for a sledge and dogs so I took the next best thing and accepted a Land Rover. But that was in the future.

As we drove along none of us said very much, Reuben because he was in pain, me from anxiety that we would get stuck (which we didn't) and Frank because he wasn't a talker. The journey was slow and tedious but eventually we arrived in Tunford street. The ambulance was waiting and as we thundered up the crew got out. We were a quarter of an hour late.

"Where have you been?" asked the ambulance driver as I climbed stiffly out of the tractor cab.

"Reuben kept wanting to stop for a pee," I quipped.

My patient heard the remark but, like Queen Victoria, he was not amused. The poor devil was hunched up in the driving seat of the tractor with a face creased with pain.

"Never mind," I told him. "It will be a lot more comfortable in the ambulance."

In no time at all the ambulancemen got him out of the tractor and loaded him onto the stretcher in the back of their vehicle. They covered him up with several blankets.

"Thanks, Doc," he shouted just before they closed the door on him.

"That's all right," I said. "Any time."

The ambulance drove off and I was left with a distinct sense of anticlimax.

"Come and have a drink," I shouted up to Frank in the tractor. He needed no second bidding. He stopped the engine and climbed down. We both walked across the street in the half light of early morning. I opened the door of the surgery cottage and we walked in. Our wall clock showed that the time was six thirty. I could scarcely believe it but I had been out for six hours doing a call that would normally have taken me half an hour at the most.

Frances had heard the commotion in the street and with marvellous anticipation she already had bacon and eggs sizzling in the frying pan. She refused a drink so I poured just Frank and myself a large glass of brandy each. And as we sipped it I related the saga of our night out in the snow to my sympathetic wife.

I don't know if I exaggerated my sufferings. Perhaps I did. But whether I exaggerated or not, my wife's Christmas present to me that year was something which I certainly wished I had had with me during the rigours of my night out in the cold. It was a pair of long woollen underpants.

14

The snow was still three inches deep on the ground but it was melting rapidly. And a good job too, I thought. Since my night out with Reuben Scase and his dislocated shoulder I had come to hate the snow. I had kitted myself up a bit better against it though. There was now a shovel in the boot of the car and I also had a 'survival pack' which was an old rucksack stuffed with two extra pullovers, some woollen socks, a large plastic bivouac bag and a thermos flask full of hot soup. Never again would I treat the elements lightly, and when the children in Tunford whooped with delight at each fresh fall of snow, Dr. Slater was just filled with a deeper sense of impending doom.

Several vehicles must have been up to the farm before me that morning. The track had been churned into a muddy slush which sprayed out satisfyingly on both sides of the car as it went along. It was Boxing Day and I had been called out to see William Barradell. I knew it must have been an urgent matter because the Barradells weren't 'senders' and would certainly not be bothering me on Boxing Day for nothing.

William was the sort of man you saw in their droves every market day in Angleton. He was in his mid sixties and given to comfortable old tweed suits, briar pipes and flat cloth caps. He had lived at Warren Farm for thirty years or more and he still did, although he no longer farmed it. He was a widower and he had retired from farming not long after his wife had died four years before. The farm had been handed over to his son Walter, lock, stock and barrel. The transfer of power had been relatively smooth but not all that voluntary. These old farmers like to hang on as long as they can, but in William's case there were medical reasons why he shouldn't. He suffered from rheumatic heart disease and had a diseased mitral valve. The cardiologists had seen him but he had been rejected for surgery. He had done very well on digoxin and diuretic tablets, but he just hadn't been capable of running the farm any more. He hadn't got the breath for it. William was a regular attender at the surgery where he came for his tablets and a check-up with the doctor about every three months. I had seen him three days before Christmas. He had complained of a cough with yellow coloured sputum.

"You've got a touch of bronchitis," I said when I had examined him. I'll give you some antibiotics and perhaps you would come and see me in three or four days time?"

"But three days will be Christmas Eve and four Christmas Day," he replied. "Can't we leave it till after Christmas?"

"Well, yes, I suppose so," I said. He took the prescription I handed him and went to wait in the dispensary queue. It was a long one, as it always was before Christmas. The regulars seemed to think that we were going to shut down for a month rather than three days and they piled in as though they were laying in for a siege. I expect the phenomenon is well known in the grocery trade too, but I have never understood it.

Mr. Barradell was still waiting in the queue when I finished surgery and the last I had seen of him was when we had exchanged nods as I had left to do my morning calls.

In the few days before Christmas we had been very busy and I hadn't given William and his bronchitis another thought. On Christmas Day I had been off duty and like a lot of other people Frances and I had eaten too much, drunk too much and watched too much television. Our daughter Sally was too young to know what the festival was all about, and my wife and I didn't feel that we had enough time off to visit either set of parents, so we had been on our own. Tunford itself had been dead, with everyone confined to their houses doing much the same as ourselves. We hadn't even seen Timothy because he had some friends visiting him and he seemed to want to keep them to himself.

So all in all I wasn't sorry to be working again on Boxing Day. I had received five calls that morning but I was visiting

William first because his had sounded the most urgent request. I hadn't liked the anxious tone in Mary Barradell's voice over the telephone. It sounded as if the old boy was much worse and I might even have to send him into hospital.

I stopped the car in the farmyard. I think one of the things which points out a good farmer is a well concreted yard. It gives the visitor a good impression right from the start, and it saves the farmer's family from continually having to live with muck and filth. It's great for the children too, because in good weather there's always plenty of space to roller skate and ride their bikes. The Barradells' yard was concreted and what's more a good part of it had already been brushed clear of snow that morning. My gum boots were an almost unnecessary luxury as I made my way to the back door. Like everyone else the Barradells had a perfectly good front door but few people in the country seemed to use them. It was only on the new housing estates and in one or two of the grander country houses where front doors were in regular use.

Warren Farm looked as if it had grown naturally out of the countryside. It fitted into it perfectly. It was a traditional timber framed, long and narrow house of the sixteenth or seventeenth century and the thatched roof kept it cool in summer and warm in winter. Over the years bits had been added — the lean-to kitchen for instance, and the interior of the whole place had been completely modernised when Walter and his wife Mary had taken the place over. The most notable improvement had been the oil fired central heating system which made the place thoroughly comfortable.

But none of this had altered the feeling which the house had of eternal peace. Like a lot of these old places it had a happy atmosphere and you could imagine generations of people like the Barradells, good sons and daughters of the soil, living in the farmhouse and tilling the land for generation after generation. Here there were no marks of musket balls on the walls, no signs of rape and pillage like those you might see when shown round an old Norman castle. This was an Anglo-Saxon place, gentle and peaceful.

Mary Barradell opened the door before I had a chance to knock. She was in her mid thirties, a pleasant, plump, farmer's wife with a fringe of dark hair and glasses. She was a jolly lass normally and I liked her. Unlike many a daughter-in-law in her situation she hadn't pestered William to get out of the house and find a bungalow for himself; she had looked after him very well for the past four years and there was a touching bond of affection between her and the old man. Perhaps that's why this morning her face was creased with worry.

"Oh hello, Doctor," she said. "Thank you for coming so quickly. I don't think he's very well at all. His cough is a lot worse and he's been going very blue at times."

"That doesn't sound too good," I said. "Where is he?"

"He's in the small sitting room. We made a bed up for him in there so he could watch the television and join in some of the Christmas fun."

"Right," I said. "Lead on MacDuff."

I followed her through the kitchen and then down a passage to the little sitting room. The whole house was beautifully warm. William certainly wouldn't be suffering from hypothermia in here, I thought. We entered the sickroom. To my surprise there was a log fire burning in the grate, but I am sure it was for appearances only because it was hardly necessary in that house. The room was gaily decorated. Coloured streamers looped their way across the ceiling and sprigs of holly had been stuck around the picture frames. In the corner a small Christmas tree was covered with tinsel. A plump little fairy doll tied to the uppermost branch of the tree bore a striking resemblance to Mary Barradell, dressed differently of course and without the glasses. But the cherubic look was there.

And to complete the picture, through the south facing

window I could see a robin pecking away at some food which had been placed on a rustic bird table just outside. It all looked very seasonal.

William was comfortably propped up with four or five pillows behind him. The little single bed looked perfectly adequate and it was obvious that every effort had been made to make him comfortable and to entertain him. But the poor old boy wasn't in a condition to appreciate any of the comfort ever again. He was dead. My first glance told me that but I didn't say so straightaway. Instead I took out my stethoscope and listened for his heartbeat. You couldn't be too careful. There was a classic case in Tunford of how Dr. Long had been called to see a man who had blown himself up while trying to undo the string on a parcel of gunpowder with a candle. When Dr. Long arrived he found the patient lying on his kitchen floor with his face all blackened.

"He's dead," said Dr. Long after a cursory look.

"No I'm not," said the man raising his head from the floor.

"Lie down, George," said the patient's brother. "Doctor knows best."

But William Barradell most certainly was dead. There was no sound coming from his heart and his eyes were fixed and dilated.

I could see by now that Mary Barradell suspected the worst.

"I'm afraid he's gone," I said.

"Oh no, Doctor," she said, tears welling up in her eyes. "He was talking to me only a few minutes before you came. I didn't think he was that bad."

"He must have had pneumonia," I said.

My own guilt surged up inside me. Why hadn't I seen him again sooner despite the holiday? Why hadn't I sent him into hospital? It was all useless but I went through it nevertheless.

"I told him to send for me straightaway if he got worse," I said, biting my lower lip. I was quite angry with myself.

"Well, I wanted to have one of you in yesterday, Doctor,"

111

she said, "but he wouldn't hear of it."

"Why ever not?" I asked.

"Because it was Christmas. He didn't want to spoil the Doctor's Christmas," she replied.

15

"There's a Mrs. Brown says she must speak to you," said Mrs. Runbelow over the telephone extension. "It's about her daughter and she says it's urgent."

I groaned. That probably meant a visit. And there's nothing more calculated to corrode a GP's arteries than a request for a visit during a busy evening surgery. Timothy was away on a two-day refresher course and all the sniffling humanity in the waiting room was my responsibility. As usual in early February, we were packed to the gunwales.

"OK," I sighed. "Put her through."

"Is that Dr. Slater?" said an anxious female voice as soon as we had been connected.

"Speaking."

"Thank goodness. It's about my daughter Jenny. I think she's in labour and I've just found out."

"Didn't you know she was pregnant?" I asked. My stomach was rapidly screwing itself into a tight little ball. I smelled danger.

"Well no, I didn't. I had been nagging her to see Dr. Bacon about a diet. But she's only just told me she's pregnant."

I took the address.

"I'll be with you in a few minutes," I said. But in the meantime could you ring for the ambulance too, please? We'll try to get her to hospital." I rang off.

"Sorry, I've got to go," I said to the patient lying on my couch. "It's an urgent call. I don't think there's much wrong with you. I'll give you a prescription for some stomach medicine. Come and see me next week.'

I wrote Mist. Mag. Trisilicate 10 mls t.d.s. Mitte 300 mls on a prescription form and handed it over. Then I was off.

As usual in the Tunford surgery the thin walls of the consulting room had held nothing from the ears in the waiting room. Everyone knew why I was going out and who I was going to. So much for medical confidentiality. The crowd in the waiting room had already begun to disperse as I charged through. One or two of the patients might possibly take a chance and wait to see if I returned. But the rest of them would be back the next day or not at all. It was always interesting to see how many people's symptoms of ill health disappeared when they were left to marinate in them for twenty four hours.

It was dark outside but my car was at the kerbside. I jumped in it and drove off like a madman in the direction of the Browns' house. Mrs. Brown was a divorcee and she and her seventeen year old daughter lived in a bungalow on the outskirts of Tunford. The place had originally been built for a retired farmer and for this reason was named 'Dunfarmin'. But the farmer and his wife had both been tragically killed in a road accident within a month of moving there, and that's how Mrs. Brown had come to buy the house. As a matter of fact Jenny and her mother were both patients of Timothy's but I had learned most of what I knew about them from Frances. It was sometimes useful to have an extra pair of eyes and ears working for you.

Mrs. Brown opened the door of 'Dunfarmin' as I drew up outside. The front garden wasn't very large and I was soon up the garden path.

"Thank you for coming so quickly, Doctor," she said. The hall was brightly lit and I could see that Mrs. Brown's careworn face was crinkled up with anxiety.

"That's all right," I said. "Where is she?"

"Through in the bedroom here." I followed her with a pounding heart. My arrival may have done something to soothe Mrs. Brown's nerves but it had done nothing for me. She had sensibly made the daughter put on a nightdress and get into bed.

With barely a 'Hello' to introduce myself I threw back the bedclothes to expose the girl's perineum. At that moment the patient was squealing and writhing about in pain, and to my horror it was perfectly obvious that labour was far advanced. The baby's head was already in view. My mouth went dry. A few minutes ago I had been grinding my way through a thoroughly dull surgery full of coughs, colds and indigestion. Now I was suddenly confronted with this. It was nearly more than my system could stand.

"Did you call the ambulance?" I asked.

"Yes, shortly after I rang you," replied Mrs. Brown.

"Well, I don't think they're going to get here in time," I said. "Can you get me some old newspapers and . . ." But my voice trailed away in horror. The lights had gone out.

"Good God!" I said. "A power cut."

Jenny screamed as the pain got worse. I dropped my medical bag and groped for the perineum to try and control the delivery of the baby's head.

"Find a torch," I shouted to Mrs. Brown.

"Will a candle do?" she asked.

"Yes, yes, anything. But for goodness sake hurry," I replied.

To me it seemed an age, even an ice age, before Mrs. Brown came into the room with a lighted candle in her hand. But it was probably only a couple of minutes really, and by the time I could see again Jenny's pain had gone off slightly. The baby's head was still inside the vagina and it had retracted slightly. Jenny lay and whimpered. The poor girl was frightened stiff. Who wouldn't be? I certainly was and my life wasn't even at risk.

"Don't worry, lassie," I said. "It's all happened before. Everything's going to be all right." But my voice sounded hollow, even to me.

Mrs. Brown lit another couple of candles and I took my coat off, rolled up my sleeves and dug around in my midder bag for some instruments. Among the rest I took out a plastic sucker and my infant laryngoscope. I had an almost medieval superstition about my laryngoscope. I believed that if I went through a ritual of checking the light bulb and laying the instrument out where I could easily grab it if the baby needed rescusitating, there would be no trouble. I did it all now. The small light bulb came on when I worked the switch, and I sighed with relief. At least I could deal with one of the possible emergencies. But what if she bled or the baby got stuck? Here in the candlelight it would be very difficult to do anything. But I hadn't much time to ponder. The next powerful uterine contraction was just starting.

Jenny had never been to an antenatal clinc or a relaxation class in her life. Nobody had told her what to expect. But now Mother Nature was saying to her that she must get rid of that baby, and that's exactly what she was going to do. She yelled and the uterine muscle pushed. Guided by my unwashed (but hopefully relatively clean) hands the baby's head was slowly extruded through the stretched circle of the mother's vulva. The delivered head then rotated a quarter of a turn of its own accord. There was a short pause, another strong contraction, and then I helped the anterior shoulder through. The rest followed easily and within seconds there was a live female infant lying between her mother's legs. The baby cried almost immediately. It was a sweet sound for it meant that the race was half won. And no fences down yet either. The mother's perineum had only suffered a slight graze; she wouldn't need any stitches.

"It's a girl," I said. But there was no joy at this birth. Jenny just wept. I went through the routine of clearing out the baby's air passages with my sucker and then I clamped the umbilical cord with two pairs of Spencer Wells forceps. I took out my scissors and cut the cord.

"Can you get something to wrap her in, please Mrs. Brown?" I said. Jenny's mother went to a chest of drawers.

"That bottom drawer would make an excellent cot," I said.

She took the drawer out and emptied the stuff out of it.

116

Then she sorted out a small white sheet; it may have been the very one Jenny was wrapped in when she was born. I handed the baby to her and she wrapped it up in the sheet. Mrs. Brown was in her own country now. She put a small blanket in the bottom of the drawer and then put the baby in it, tucking her up with another little blanket on top. All this had been done on the edge of the bed.

"Good," I said. "Now put the drawer on the floor and then place a big book under the bottom end so that the baby's head is tilted down slightly. That helps all the mucus to drain out of the air passages."

She did what I asked. Mrs. Brown seemed to be a very capable and practical person. It augured well for Jenny's future. It didn't look as if her mother would be the sort to make her daughter suffer for what she had done.

While Mrs. Brown had been sorting out the baby I had tried to keep my manner as cool and calm as I could. But in reality I was still very worried. I always was until the placenta was out, because a retained placenta is the nightmare of any obstetrician, especially those who practise domiciliary obstetrics. If a woman has a bleed in hospital it is relatively easy to set up a drip and give her some blood; it's also quite easy to take her to theatre and remove the retained placenta which is the cause of her bleeding. But at home all this is ten times more difficult, even if you have the facilities on hand. And the facilities can be on hand. For many years hospitals have organised domiciliary flying squads, and if the GP requests it he can have a team of experts out to help him deal with most of the frightening complications of obstetrics. But you didn't send out an S.O.S. until you were in real trouble and for the moment I wasn't. The blood loss was only very slight.

I waited, but nothing happened. Jenny had a little pain but it came to nothing. The placenta stayed where it was. Mrs. Brown had now fixed me up with a pudding bowl and some newspapers and I was all ready to catch the afterbirth. But the only trouble was it didn't seem to want to be caught.

I took the patient's blood pressure. It was 210/120 — sky high. My heart leapt into my mouth. I couldn't believe this was all happening to me. The thing which obstetricians probably dread more than anything else is toxaemia, the prevention of which is what all that blood pressure taking and urine testing in antenatal care is all about. And a blood pressure that high must mean that Jenny had pre-eclampsia. She could have had a fit and died on me any time since I had come into the house.

"Can I use your phone, please?" I asked Mrs. Brown.

"Certainly, Doctor. It's in the hall," she said.

She handed me a candle on a saucer. It was one of those wide-based 'night lights' and I didn't have to do any balancing acts with it as I found my way to the telephone. I picked up the receiver and rang the Angleton General.

"Is Mr. MacDonald in the hospital?" I asked when the man on the switchboard answered.

"Yes, as a matter of fact he is," he said. "I think he's in the labour ward. I'll put you through." I heard him ring the ward and then the staff nurse's voice answered. She called Hector MacDonald to the phone. I had never been more pleased to hear his steady Scots voice, and I felt like doing a penance for the time when I had nearly fallen asleep in one of his postgraduate lectures.

"Hello," I said. "It's Corney Slater from Tunford. I've got a slight problem," I said with what I thought was convincing English understatement.

"Yes, what is it?"

"We've had a power cut here," I said, "and I've just been called to a seventeen year old primip. who has had no antenatal care. I managed to deliver the baby by candlelight but she seems to have a retained placenta. There's been no bleeding but the worst thing of all is that her blood pressure is 210/120."

He clicked his tongue.

"Goodness. You do find them don't you," he said. "But if she's not bleeding there's no point in the flying squad coming out to work in the dark. We still have power here in Angleton, and even if it does go off the hospital has an emergency generator. So the best thing you can do is bring her in. I suggest you set up a drip and give her whatever you've got in your bag to get her blood pressure down. And while you're about it what about a tranquilliser for yourself?"

"That won't be necessary," I said airily (like hell it wasn't). "But thanks a lot. I'll see you soon."

As I put the telephone down there was a knock on the front door. The ambulance had arrived; I opened the door and let the men in.

"What's happened to the lights?" they asked.

"We've had a power cut," I replied. "And I'm glad to see you I can tell you, the baby's here but we've got a retained placenta on our hands. I'm going to take her in. I don't want to delay you but I want to set up a drip before we move her."

"OK Doc," they said. One of the men was carrying a flashlight. He switched it on and followed me back to the bedroom.

Things were much as they had been.

"The ambulance is here," I announced. "And I've had a word with the obstetrician at the hospital," I said. "He thinks it's best if we take you into hospital to have the afterbirth removed. But before we shift you I'm going to set up a drip in your arm."

Jenny nodded and bit her lower lip. I had spoken to her directly and had tried to sound confident, but I wasn't sure quite how it had come out.

"Don't worry," I added. "We'll soon get you out of this mess."

She didn't look too sure, but I decided to cut the cackle and get on with the job. When I had been a houseman I had been something of a consultant dripologist; other doctors would often call me to set up infusions on their patients when they had failed. Setting up drips was a skill, perhaps the only one, at

119

which I had been a little over the average in ability. But it was like being a good darts player. You need practice to stay good at it. And in general medical practice the chance to set up a drip comes once in a blue moon. I certainly hadn't done it since I had left hospital. What's more I had never done it in a patient's home by the light of an electric torch and with my hands trembling with anxiety because I knew what a terrible thing it would be if I muffed it.

Jenny was shivering slightly. The heating had gone off with the power, and it could have been just that which was making her shiver. But it could also have been the first sign of an eclamptic fit. I unpacked my drip set and a bottle of dextrose saline from my bag as quickly as I could and to my relief I hit the vein with the needle first time. I got one of the ambulancemen to play 'drip stand' and hold the bottle of dextrose saline in the air while I connected it to the giving set. I let the fluid dribble onto the carpet until I had excluded all the air bubbles and then I plugged the 'male' end of the plastic tubing of the giving set into the 'female' connection on the needle in the patient's arm. I made the tubing into a loop and then anchored it to Jenny's forearm with some sticking plaster. The idea of the loop was that if the drip was pulled upon there would be some give in the line before it was wrenched out of the vein. It was a useful dodge, and might save us from disaster. For if Jenny did bleed and we arrived at the hospital with an exsanguinating patient, my drip would be the only route through which the hospital boys would be able to give blood.

I fiddled with the control valve on the giving set until I had reduced the flow to a slow drip in the counting chamber. My luck was holding. The patient still hadn't bled and she still hadn't had a fit. I found some intravenous Largactil and Pethidine in my bag and broke open the vials. Then with a plastic syringe and a No. 1 needle I sucked up the contents of both vials and squirted the cocktail into the patient's blood stream through the drip set cannula. I thought that the two drugs would help sedate her and possibly reduce her blood pressure while we made the trip, but I wasn't over hopeful.

"Right," I said to the ambulancemen. "You can shift her now."

I took the bottle from the drip stand man. His colleague had been out to the ambulance while I had been setting up the drip, and he had returned with a two wheeled trolley. Within a few minutes all of us, Jenny, Mrs. Brown, the baby, myself and the two ambulancemen had packed into the ambulance and were hurtling towards Angleton with the siren going and the blue light flashing. When we got to Angleton the only person who seemed to be the worse for wear was myself. I had my old problem of motion sickness. But Jenny and the baby were fine.

Hector MacDonald himself met us at the door of the obstetric unit and a few minutes later Jenny was whipped into theatre to have the placenta removed under a general anaesthetic.

She never looked back and a few days later she decided to have the baby adopted. But that was in the future. For the time being my job was done and I felt a sudden sense of uselessness. I had handed over to my consultant colleague and that was that. Mrs. Brown was in the waiting room and I went to say goodbye to her. Then I persuaded one of the midwives to drive me back to Tunford. She drove nice and slowly and I wasn't feeling at all sick when she dropped me off and I picked up my car.

I went back to the surgery. I had been away just over two hours but nevertheless there were still three people waiting to see me. All of them had trivial complaints and had probably stuck out the wait partly to spite Mr. Somerville who had done his best to shift them off home. But I soon dispatched them and then I went into the flat to tell Frances what had been happening.

"Funny," she said, when I had poured it all out. "I saw Jenny Brown in the village yesterday and I thought then that she was pregnant. I meant to tell you about it but I forgot."

16

"What's the matter?" I asked.

"That's what I want you to tell me," he replied.

I bit my lip. The surgery was packed out and I was extremely busy, but there was no excuse for me to have given him such an easy chance to get the better of me. At medical school they had always taught us to say 'What seems to be the trouble?', and although the phrase had seemed ponderous at the time, there was obvious sense in using it. Especially when you came up against smart Alecs like this. Perhaps it was because he was a Yorkshireman, but Robert Dingle was far more cocky than the locals. He had the self confidence of a man who has moved about a bit, and his self confidence was nowhere more obvious than on the cricket field. In two short seasons he had become Tunford's star batsman and wicket keeper. But his prowess on the cricket field didn't impress me particularly. My father had been so keen on the sport that I had behaved like many a son and reacted completely against it. I paid my subscription as a Vice President of the Tunford Cricket Club, but that was only because the secretary had tapped me for a quid or two because I was a local 'dignitary'. I had never been to one of their games because, quite frankly, cricket bored me.

"OK," I sighed. "I'll rephrase that. Of what are you complaining?"

"I've had a terrible cough for about three days," he said.

"Open your mouth," I said.

He did so and I put my thermometer under his tongue.

"Close you mouth but don't bite it," I said, just like I did with the children. I was back with the psychological advantage. There would now be at least half a minute's silence while the thermometer brewed.

I looked towards the window. The bottom three quarters of the consulting room window were of frosted glass to stop passers-by peering in. But the top quarter was clear and I could see that it was still raining quite heavily. The water collected round the bottom of the small circular ventilation panel which was set into the clear part of the glass, and every now and then a rivulet of water would detach itself from the tiny reservoir which had been created and go trickling down the length of the panel. It didn't look like the weather to be out in, especially if you were an agricultural representative like Robert. The farmers wouldn't be in a very good mood in this.

When I thought the thermometer had brewed I took it out of his mouth. The mercury stood at one hundred and two degrees Fahrenheit. It certainly didn't look as if he was malingering.

"You've got a temperature all right," I said. "Let's have a look down your throat then."

He opened his mouth. I depressed his tongue with a wooden spatula and shone my pen torch at his pharynx. It seemed a bit red but apart from that there was nothing abnormal. There were no signs of tonsillitis and neither were there any of the small petechial haemorrhages on the palate which I had learnt to associate with glandular fever.

"This cough of yours. Is it productive?" I asked.

"What do you mean?"

"Are you bringing any phlegm up?"

"Yes, a little."

"What colour is it?"

"Pale yellow."

"I see," I said. "Can you take your jacket off and pull up your shirt please."

He did as I had asked and I plugged my stethoscope into my ears and listened to his chest. There were one or two squeaks but nothing else. No reduced air entry which might suggest lung consolidation.

I finished and told him to tuck his shirt back into his trousers. He did so.

"Well, I think it's only a touch of the 'flu," I said. "Go straight to bed, take some aspirin and drink plenty of fluids. And because this cough seems to be a bit productive I think I will give you an antibiotic. I'll give you a certificate for a week off work. Come and see me at the end of that time if all goes according to plan. But if you don't feel a lot better in two or three days let me know."

I wrote out a certificate and a prescription for a five day course of Tetracycline and handed both bits of paper to the patient.

"Thanks Doc," he said. I pressed the buzzer for the next patient and he was gone. By the end of that morning Robert as an individual had gone from my memory too. There were several more people with similar symptoms who came after him and they all merged into a oneness. It looked as if a 'flu epidemic was starting up, and that is no joke for a GP. I have lived through one great 'flu epidemic and it's no fun. That is if you don't regard forty or fifty calls a day as fun, and most of us wouldn't.

But this time it fizzled out. The epidemic was a fairly minor affair and three days after I had seen Robert the visiting book was still looking pretty average for the time of year.

I looked through the book after surgery. Timothy had put his initials against visits he had intended to do and I had to pick up the rest. My partner was always scrupulously fair to me and I noticed that he had taken more than half. But right in the middle of the page was Robert Dingle's name.

"What does he want a visit for?" I asked the receptionist.

"Oh, he rang to say his temperature was still up and his cough hadn't gone yet. He said you had told him to ring if he wasn't any better," said Mrs. Runbelow.

"Yes, so I did," I replied.

Timothy and I had coffee together as usual in his kitchen. We discussed the 'flu 'epidemic' and decided that thankfully it looked as if it was going to be a damp squib. It was a cheering thought and I was in quite a good mood when I drove up to Robert's place twenty minutes later. The Yorkshireman was a bachelor but nevertheless he had had the good sense to buy himself a bungalow when he had moved to the area. It has always seemed a waste of money to me to pay rent on a place if you can afford to purchase, and there was no doubt that Robert could afford a mortgage. He had a good job and no ties.

The house was a bungalow on a small new estate development in Kingtree. It wouldn't have been to my taste because there was hardly any garden and the neighbours were too close. But for Robert it was ideal. He certainly didn't want to spend all his Saturday afternoons in the summer mowing the lawn, and the neighbours were a matter of indifference to him. I parked the car and walked to the front door. It was unlocked so I turned the handle and walked right in.

"Hello," I shouted. "Where are you?"

"In here," shouted a croaky voice from behind a partially closed door. I went in. There was a real fug in the bedroom — the smell of sweat, unwashed socks and illness. Robert was lying in his bed and he looked rough. Just like I did sometimes after Rugby Club dinners — unshaven, red eyed and haggard. The effort of saying, 'come in' had set him going on another little coughing spasm and I waited for it to subside.

"How do you feel?" I asked.

"How does it look?" he replied.

"Not very good," I said. "Have you been drinking a lot of fluids as I told you?"

"Yes," he said. "And taking the tablets. But I think I'm heading the same way as the parrot."

I didn't understand.

"What do you mean?" I asked.

"Well, me bloody parrot died yesterday," he said. "The vet's doing a post mortem today."

My ears pricked up.

125

"How long have you had the parrot?" I asked.

"About ten days, that's all," he replied. "It cost me twenty five quid. I'm going to sue that bloody pet shop if I can. Twenty five quid and the thing cocks its clogs up the very next week. It's not good enough." He started off on another paroxysm of coughing.

The little cogwheels inside my brain began to whir and the tickertape spelled out psittacosis. It was a rare disease in human beings, the books said, but some imported birds, like parrots and budgerigars, sometimes carried it. I raked around my brain for the symptoms and signs. High fever but low pulse rate, and a cough caused by the pneumonitis was all I could think of.

"I had better examine you," I said. "Can you take your pyjama top off, please?"

I went over him very thoroughly. His temperature was one hundred and one degrees Fahrenheit, pulse rate seventy two per minute (that fitted). When I listened to his chest there were a few crackles in the right mid zone which would be consistent with a pneumonitis.

I finished and straightened up.

"I think you have got psittacosis," I said.

"What the hell's that," said Robert.

"It's a viral illness which you catch off parrots. It causes inflammation of the lungs. And as a matter of fact, quite by chance, I have put you on one of the few antibiotics which does any good for it."

"Well, it doesn't seem to have done much good yet," he said.

"No, but that may be because I haven't given it in high enough doses. We need to double up the tablets. And I would like to get an X-ray and blood tests done as well. Could you get someone to nip you into the hospital today? I'm sure a quick trip in and out will do you no harm, and it would help a great deal with the diagnosis."

"Oh yes. Someone from the cricket club will drive me in,

I'm sure. I know one or two people who are hanging around with nothing much to do," he replied.

"Good," I said. "And you mentioned that the vet was doing a post mortem on the parrot today. Which vet was it?"

"Mr. McIver," he replied.

"Well, it might be a good idea if I had a word with him. Can I use your telephone?" I asked.

"Feel free. It's in the sitting room. McIver's number's on the pad."

"Thanks," I said.

I walked through to the sitting room and rang the vets' surgery. A young female voice answered. It sounded like one of their dolly bird receptionists. Mrs. Runbelow would probably have been able to give her forty years. But perhaps that wasn't a bad thing, because dolly birds weren't always noted for their efficiency.

"Hello," I said. "Dr. Slater here. Can I speak to Mr. McIver, please?"

"Sorry, he's out," she said. "But if it's important I can get him on the radio and ask him to ring you back."

Show off, I thought. But I said, "Well as a matter of fact it is rather important so perhaps you could do just that please. I'm at Kingtree 285."

"Thank you," she said, and rang off. I put the receiver down and went back into the bedroom to chat with Robert. About three minutes later the telephone rang and I answered it.

"Oh hello, Corney," said Duncan's voice at the other end. What can I do you for? Stuck with a calving or something are you?"

"No," I replied. "It's about Robert Dingle's parrot. What did it die of?"

"Well, I haven't done any fancy tests yet, but I'm sure it had psittacosis," he said. "Why do you ask?"

"I think Robert's got it too."

He whistled through his teeth. "Oh has he?" he said. "A friend of mine at veterinary college died of it, you know."

127

"You're cheerful," I said. "It can happen of course, but I think he should be all right on the Tetracycline. He's a big tough chap. And Tetracycline is marvellous stuff."

"I do agree," he said.

"Well, thanks very much," I said. "I'll go and pass on the good news."

I replaced the receiver and went back to my patient.

"It looks as if the parrot did have psittacosis," I said.

"Oh bloody marvellous," said Robert. "Just you wait till I get my hands on that pet shop owner."

"I think you will have to be fit before you do anything like that," I said. "Now let's get the paperwork done."

I wrote out a prescription for more Tetracycline tablets, and then filled in the blood test and X-ray request forms. When I had explained all about them I left them on Robert's bedside table.

"Right, I'll see you tomorrow," I said. "This is quite exciting, you know. I don't think we've ever had a case of psittacosis in Tunford before."

"Big deal," said Robert, and I realised how inappropriate the remark had been. A doctor's scientific enthusiasm may often make him forget that he is dealing with human beings.

I apologised and left to do the rest of my calls. The next day I visited Robert again. He seemed a little better. The day after that he was better still and within ten days he was cured.

The X-rays and blood tests confirmed the diagnosis, and the results added fuel to the indignation burning in Robert's breast. He had been helped through his illness by modern medicine but I don't think he felt that that was anything to be grateful about. What he was worried about was the twenty five quid he had lost on the parrot.

I didn't envy that pet shop owner.

17

"She's a most immoral ladeee
She's a most immoral ladeeeeee
She's a most immoral ladeeeeeeeeee"

The words of the famous Rugby song bounced off the walls of the clubhouse at a volume fit to split your eardrums. John Copsey, our full back, had announced his intention of getting married the next week and the rest of the club hadn't needed much encouragement to stage a party for the poor chap. The evening had been a great success. That is if you judged success by the amplitude of the singing, the density of the cigarette smoke in the atmosphere and the amount of spilled beer on the floor. But not all the beer had gone on the floor by any means. The future bridegroom had sunk at least seven pints and most of the rest of the team weren't far behind. I counted myself lucky that I had been a late arrival and had only managed to down a modest three pints, and I watched with some misgivings as John drained his glass and plonked it on the bar counter to be refilled. I suddenly thought that perhaps I shouldn't have been so rash as to offer him a lift home in our car, but it had seemed churlish not to do so when Frances had been coming into Angleton to get me anyway, and John lived in the village of Hickforth which was on our way home.

"And she got between the sheets
with nothing on at all . . ."

There was raucous laughter as the song came to an end. Just then there were three blasts on a car horn outside the clubhouse. That was my signal. Frances didn't care to set foot in the clubhouse with everyone in their cups, and I must say I didn't blame her.

I tapped John on the shoulder.

"Come on," I said. "The taxi's here."

"Oh no. Not already," he said. "Can't she wait till I've finished me pint at least?"

"If you must," I said. "But I think you've had quite enough already. Make it quick if you don't want to walk home."

John put the fresh pint to his lips and downed it without taking a breath. For such a small chap, and at this stage of the evening too, it really was a remarkable effort.

"Right," he said. "I'm ready." He turned round to the company to say goodbye, but nobody took any notice because although his impending marriage had been the reason for the get together, the future groom was now an irrelevance. The party had taken on its own rowdy momentum and most people were too interested in a disturbance that was going on at the other end of the room to pay any heed to Mr. Copsey. The drunken full back and his doctor friend slipped quietly out of the door. And perhaps just in time, for I had a feeling that this was becoming an unsuitable place for a member of the medical profession. It was difficult enough for a doctor to maintain his dignity in a Rugby Club anyway, but if he got too involved in this sort of thing his reputation might quickly plumb unheard of depths of disrepute.

Outside the night air was cool and refreshing. Frances was sitting in the car quite near the clubhouse door and the driving window was down.

"Hello," she said when she saw me. "Where's John?"

I turned round. I thought my friend had been hot behind me, but all I could see now was a crumpled form lying in the porch of the clubhouse. The fresh air had been too much for him.

"Oh God, it looks as if he's passed out," I said.

Frances got out of the car and went over to him.

"Is he all right?" she asked.

"I think so," I replied. "He's just a little over the odds. Why can't these guys learn to say no."

"You're a fine one to talk," commented my wife with a laugh.

I slapped John's face but the only response was a low moan. It didn't look as if he was going to make it to the car under his own steam.

"I'll get help," I said.

I went back into the clubhouse. Peter Dawson and Alec Brown were standing just inside the door. They were both sensible chaps and they were showing little interest in the shenanigans at the other end of the bar.

"Can you give me a lift with Copsey," I said. "He's flaked out just outside."

"Sure, Corney," they said, and followed me.

John was still flat out on the floor.

"Hop in the car," I said to Frances. "I don't want you injuring your back. We can manage this lump." Frances got in the driving seat again and we three men carried the unconscious Copsey to the car and dumped him in the back seat.

"Sweet dreams," said Peter as we shut the door.

"Thanks a lot," I said to my two helpers. "We'd better get a move on before he starts being sick." They laughed and I hopped into the front passenger seat of the car. Frances started the car and we moved off at a steady pace.

Ten minutes or so later we stopped outside John's digs. It was a house on one of the new private housing estates which they were building in most of the villages close to Angleton. There were garish yellow coloured street lights all over the estate. I noticed that the garden in front of Mr. Copsey's domicile was still bare earth, but nevertheless the garden gnomes had already moved in.

I turned round to my friend.

"Here we are, John," I shouted, but there was no response. I nudged him and shook him but there was no response. Judging by the comfortable snores he was emitting it seemed as if he was out for the night. After a few moments indecision I got out of the car and knocked on the landlady's door. A severe looking middle aged lady answered.

"We've brought Mr. Copsey home," I said. "I'm terribly sorry but I'm afraid he's rather the worse for wear. Hatchet-faced she followed me up the garden path. I opened the back door of our car and showed her the prostrate form in the back seat. John was still snoring away like a contented pig.

"How disgusting," she said. "You're not going to bring him into my house like that." And with that she turned on her heel, walked back into the house and slammed the door.

"The rotten old so and so," I said, and stuck my tongue out at the closed portal. I looked at Frances as I shut the car door again.

"Well, we can't leave him in the gutter," I said. "We'll have to take him home, won't we?"

She agreed. I climbed back into the car and we set off for Tunford.

When we arrived the village night life was going full swing. The fish and chip shop was doing a roaring trade and the motor bike lads and their girls were hanging around under one of the street lights. What was worse, Pedlar and his wife were sitting outside their house in their little blue van just like they often did. Pedlar was the local ratcatcher, and when he and his missus wanted entertainment in the evening they didn't switch on the telly, they just went out into the street and sat in the van watching the world go by; not much happened in Tunford without them knowing about it.

John was still oblivious to all.

"How on earth are we going to get him into the flat without that lot gawping at us?" I said. It certainly wouldn't do my image as a respectable GP much good to be seen dragging a body through my front door. If I had been taking him into the surgery it might have been all right, but the flat was a different kettle of fish altogether.

132

"How about asking Harry if he can help?" said Frances.

"Good thought," I said. "I'll go and see if he's in."

Harry Bailey was Tunford's grocer. He was a vice president of the Rugby Club and as an ex-RAF officer he knew all about drunken mess parties. What's more I could rely on him to keep his mouth shut.

Just then Pedlar and his wife got out of the van and went into their house. They must have decided that it was all a bit routine this evening and not enough was happening to justify them putting up with the cold. How wrong they were.

"That's Pedlar out of the way anyway," I said to Frances. "I expect you will have to move Sally's cot in with us and put up the spare bed. Perhaps Mrs. Yallop will help you before she goes." (Mrs. Yallop had been babysitting.)

"I've thought of all that," said Frances. "I'm not just a pretty face, you know."

We both got out of the car and went our various ways as nonchalantly as we could. As Frances disappeared into the flat, I strode down the street and knocked on Harry's door as if I did it every night. The dog round in the grocer's back yard started kicking up a hell of a racket and I shouted at it to shut up.

Harry lived in a flat over the shop just like we did and after a few moments I heard him coming down the stairs cursing. I was glad that I wasn't after a gallon of paraffin or a bar of soap. If I had been, I had the feeling that I would soon have been told where to put the said items.

"Oh hello," he said as he opened the door. "I didn't think it would be you."

"Sorry to bother you, Harry," I said, "but I've been to a party at the Rugby Club. John Copsey's in the car and he's pissed as a newt. Can you give us a lift to get him into the flat."

"Certainly, old boy," said Harry with a laugh. His grey RAF moustache bristled as if it remembered times past.

"Back in a minute love," he shouted up the stairs to his

wife. Then he joined me in the street and closed the door behind him.

We sauntered along as though we were two friends out for an evening stroll, and when we reached the car we stopped and leaned with our backs against it as though we were in some deep philosophical debate. Mrs. Yallop came out of the flat and headed for Timothy's house. We wished her goodnight, and she gave us a knowing look. I expect Frances had told her something of our predicament.

Shortly after Mrs. Yallop had gone, the motorbikes roared off in a group and there was a gap in the fish and chip shop traffic. We moved like greased lightning. I opened the door of the flat and Harry did likewise with the rear door of the car. When we both tried to lift our friend out of the back of the car he felt like a ton weight. Before, when I had manhandled him it had been with the help of two hefty Rugby forwards. But now one unfit grocer and one slightly drunk doctor didn't make the same sort of team at all. It was a lot harder work but somehow we managed to part drag and part carry the drunken form across the pavement and into the flat without being seen. Just inside the door we collapsed in a chortling heap on top of our companion. But he didn't seem to notice at all. He was still flat out. I shut the door behind us and Harry and I leaned against the walls of the passage to regain our breath.

"Jesus," I panted. "We must have looked like Burke and Hare."

"Never mind. We did it," said Harry. "Where do you want him?"

"In Sally's room," I replied. "That's up the stairs, I'm afraid."

Frances appeared on the scene.

"Yes," she said. "I've made up the bed."

"Righto," I said. "Up the stairs with him." This time I seemed to have stopped worrying about Frances' back. She helped us pull and push our drunken pig of a friend up the stairs and into Sally's room.

134

We threw him on the spare bed and took another breather. All this exertion may not have done anything for John's state of intoxication, but I had pretty well sobered up completely. My medical training began to surface at last and as I looked at the victim spreadeagled on the bed, for the first time I realised that he was deeply and dangerously anaesthetised. I pinched him but he didn't flinch. I fumbled for my pen torch and shone a light in his eyes. His pupils were moderately dilated and responded only slowly to light. A moment of cold fear gripped me. In my mind's eye I could already see the newspaper headlines screaming 'Drunk Dies in Doctor's Flat' or 'Doctor Struck Off After Drink Death.' What should I do? He really ought to go to the hospital casualty department, but even then there would be an embarassing fuss. I was just pondering all this when the patient suddenly started to vomit violently. I quickly turned him onto his side to stop him inhaling any of the vomit. When he seemed to have finished I cleaned him up as best I could with a towel which Frances had brought me.

At least the vomiting solved one problem. The beer which had come up couldn't be absorbed into his bloodstream. But if he was going to continue vomiting there was a great danger that he might inhale some of his regurgitated stomach contents. That's sometimes what has happened when you hear of drunks dying in police cells. People who are deeply anaesthetised with alcohol need just as careful nursing as anybody recovering from an operation. Somebody needs to make sure that they lie on their side and keep the airway free until the level of anaesthesia lightens sufficiently for the patient's own reflexes to take over. I decided that I would have to play nurse.

"It looks as if I'm going to have to stay with him a while," I said. I could see that Harry was rapidly losing interest, and I didn't blame him.

"Well, I'll be off," he said. "Have fun, won't you."

"Thanks Harry," I said. "And remember, mum's the word."

"Righto," he said, and was gone.

Frances saw Harry out and then came upstairs again bringing with her a bucket with some disinfectant and a cloth in it. I took it from her and did my best to clear up the vomit.

"I'll go and have a bath," said Frances.

"OK," I said. "There's no point in both of us sitting here watching him." She left and I pulled up a bedside chair and settled down to my vigil.

I heard Frances running the bath. While she was in the bath John vomited twice, and when Frances reappeared in her dressing gown with a cup of tea for me the room reeked strongly of fresh vomit. I didn't feel much like the tea but I gulped it down nevertheless.

I handed her the empty cup. "You go off to bed, dear," I said. "See you in the morning."

I don't think she needed much encouragement, but I cast an envious eye after her as she left the room. I felt very tired and I had a busy day ahead of me on the morrow. I lost enough sleep in the line of duty without messing about like this when I was off.

I began to hate the drunken animal on the bed. I noticed that he had become incontinent of urine but I was too tired and resentful to do anything about it. Let him lie in it, I thought. He vomited three or four more times but as the clock ticked on the level of anaesthesia lightened and after a couple of hours I thought it was safe to leave him. I crept away, took off my trousers and slipped into bed with my wife in my underpants and shirt.

At seven o'clock the alarm went off. I woke up feeling absolutely dreadful. My eyes were just red sockets and my mouth felt dry and filthy. In a tired rage I went into the spare room to see how my charge was doing. I shook him and he woke up.

"Good morning," I said between my teeth.

"Where am I?" he said.

"Tunford," I said. "At my house in Tunford. Your landlady wouldn't have you. And I don't blame her."

He felt the wet bedclothes around him. "Ugh," he said. "I must have been pissed."

"You were," I said. "And I don't mind telling you, you caused us some trouble."

I didn't add that but for me he might well have died, and that his was probably the first life I had saved since I had qualified. I had been waiting for this moment for a long time, but somehow I didn't feel any glow of satisfaction.

"I'll run a bath for you," I said.

I went into the bathroom and ran a tepid bath for him. Then I helped him to the bath and he slowly undressed and got in.

"God, my head feels like a ton weight," he said.

"It ought to," I replied unsympathetically.

While he had his bath I shaved. Then while he was drying himself I sorted out some dry clothes for him.

Twenty minutes later we sat down to breakfast together. The chap opposite bore hardly any resemblance to the singing buck of the night before. He looked pale and awful and the suit which I had lent him was two sizes too big. I thought that I had seen better looking scarecrows. Frances unceremoniously plonked a plateful of bacon and eggs in front of him, but with a gesture reminiscent of a well-bred lady who has just been offered a trip round a sewage works he brought his handkerchief up to his mouth and turned his head away.

"Sorry Fran," he mumbled. "I'm not hungry."

Just at that moment the telephone rang and I went to answer it. The caller was Mrs. Bunn from Kingtree.

"Could you come and see Edward, please Doctor?" she said. "He's had a pain in his tummy all night and he's been sick twice."

"Any diarrhoea?" I asked.

"No," she said.

"I'll try and come before surgery," I said.

Secretly I wasn't at all displeased at having this golden opportunity to get away from John. His company was wearing me down. I phoned Harry.

"I have to go out on a visit," I said. "Could you do me a favour, please, and run our drunken friend home?"

"Well, yes old boy," replied Harry. "How is he?"

"He'll live," I said. "But I think it will be a day or two before he touches another drop of alcohol."

I told John that Harry would be picking him up in a few moments. He seemed grateful for the news.

Then I left on my visit. Edward Bunn had appendicitis and I had to send him into hospital. It took me quite a while to arrange the admission and the ambulance and when I got back to Tunford I had to start morning surgery straightaway. I didn't go into the flat until later. When I did, John had departed long before. Frances took me upstairs to show me the spare bedroom. The room had been cleaned up but there was little she could do about the mattress on the spare bed. There was a huge indelible stain in the centre of it which would remain for ever more.

"You and your Rugby," she said.

"Well, it was the first time I've saved a life," I said. The remark was received with little or no impact.

But three days later John Copsey came up trumps. He arrived on the doorstep with my old suit which he had had cleaned in one hand, and in his other hand he held a huge bunch of flowers for my wife.

Which only goes to show that Rugby players may have some funny habits, but at the end of the day they will always behave like gentlemen.

18

"Do yew loike hare, Doctor?" asked Octavius.

"Well, er, I've never tried it Mr. Waddell," I said, sensing a gift somewhere in the offing. Timothy and I never refused gifts. They were offered rarely enough, and a free morsel for the cooking pot was more than welcome. But as usual it wasn't a rich man who was being generous but a poor old-aged pensioner who hadn't two ha'pennies to rub together. It was the old, old story. The rich were usually as mean as anything while the old boys who had never had anything would give you the shirt off their backs.

Octavius Waddell looked for all the world like those pictures of Bismarck you see in the history books. He didn't wear a helmet with a spike, of course, but the round face and white walrus moustache were there all right. Not that he would have liked to be compared to Bismarck, because as a soldier in the First World War he had been taught to hate all 'sausage eaters' and the hatred hadn't worn off. Octavius was extremely proud of his war service and a picture in his living room showed what a fine young man Trooper Waddell had been. You could hardly imagine that that strapping young fellow was now the stooped and portly old chap who lived in one of Tunford's old people's bungalows.

For the past three weeks he had been suffering from lumbago. I had merely offered sympathy and a few pain killers and let Nature do the rest, but the old boy had developed a touching faith in me and he reckoned that my pills had worked miracles.

"Wait till yew taste it, bor," he said. "Hare's lovely. Oi've got one here that moi son fetched for me yesterday. There's too much meat on it fer me and Oi wouldn't do it justice. Oi'd loike yew ter hev it."

"Well, really, I couldn't," I said.

"Yes yew can," he said. "Oi insist."

He hobbled through into his kitchen and presently returned carrying a hare by its back legs. It was a big buck and it certainly did look meaty.

"There," said Octavius. "Ain't he a booty? Do yew take him to yore little woife. She'll be pleased, that she will."

"That's very good of you Mr. Waddell," I said. "Thank you very much. I'm sure we'll enjoy it."

As I took the animal off the patient he gave it a farewell look which consumed me with guilt. I felt sure he would have liked to keep it for himself.

"Gosh, he is a big one," I said as I felt the full weight of the animal. "That's really super of you Mr. Waddell. I never expected anything like this when I walked in here today."

Octavius beamed.

"Well, I'd better be off," I said. "Let me know if the back pain returns, won't you," I said.

"Roight oh," he replied, and I left.

The animal's ears dragged on the ground as I walked to the car. Fortunately it was only a few steps and as far as I know nobody saw me put it in the boot. I didn't quite know how Octavius's son had come by the beast and I thought it was best that I behaved discreetly just in case I happened to be the receiver of stolen property.

When I arrived home I marched into the kitchen with my prize. "Look what I've got," I said triumphantly.

"What on earth's that?" replied Frances.

"It's a hare," I said. "Octavius Waddell gave it to me. I thought we might have it for supper."

"Hmmmm," she murmured unenthusiastically. "I've never cooked hare, and I couldn't gut it. You would have to do that."

The job didn't appeal to me very much. Not that I was squeamish, but all that sort of thing did remind me of the post mortem room.

140

"Oh," I said. "Tell you what then. I'll take it down to the butcher's after lunch."

"All right," said Frances. "But in the meantime could you please go and put it in the coal shed?"

"I'll do better than that," I said. "I'll put it back in the car boot."

So much for my wife being delighted. Poor old Octavius, I thought. It would have been far better if he had kept the thing for himself. After lunch I took the hare to Mr. Fisk the butcher.

"Hello, started poaching now, have we?" he said.

"No, it's a present from a patient," I said. "Can you gut it for me please?"

"Certainly. When was it shot?"

"On Saturday, I believe," I replied.

"Oh I see. Only two days ago," he said. "Well that needs to hang a bit. I'll let you know when it's ready for eating."

"Thanks," I replied. I didn't want to display my ignorance by saying that I had expected to eat it that evening. I had known that pheasants were usually hung, but where hares were concerned I was a babe in arms. I felt as stupid as the Indian registrar at the hospital must have done when his consultant ran over a pheasant in his car.

"I'll hang it for a week and then you must come over for supper," said the consultant.

"Hang it," said the registrar. "I thought it was already dead?"

I handed the animal over and left.

Just over a week later Mr. Fisk gave the skinned and gutted beast back to Frances. To tell the truth I think it came as a surprise. I think she had almost forgotten about it.

When I came in for lunch she showed it to me.

"There's your hare," she said.

The meat had a faint green colour and smelled of early decomposition. It didn't look any too appetising.

"Oh yes," I said. "Are we going to have it for supper?"

"Well, you can, if you like," she said, "but I'm not."

I thought of Octavius. "I'd like to try some anyway," I said. "Have you thought how to cook it? They jug it don't they? What does that involve?"

"Oh, that's a bit complicated," she said. "But my cookery book says you can have it grilled."

"Super," I said, trying hard not to let my resolve crack. "Are you sure you won't try it too?"

"No. Definitely not," she said.

Ah well, I thought. She is pregnant. Her fads have to be forgiven.

*

That evening I finished surgery at about seven o'clock. As a matter of fact I had chatted to one or two of the patients about hare meat during the day and they had reassured me greatly. "Oh, that's bootiful to eat," they had said licking their chops. "Oi mind the way me mother used to do 'em . . ." It all gave me encouragement and I went into the flat with my gastric juices already flowing. I felt I was in for a treat. But as soon as I was through the door I was met by a funny pungent smell. It was something between the warm smell of a maltings and the sickly sweet odour of a silage heap.

I walked through to the kitchen. Frances turned up her nose when she saw me.

"Yuk," she said. "I don't know how you can think of eating this stuff." She pulled back the grill of the oven and I took a look at the meat. She had cut off one of the animal's hind-quarters and it was now about half cooked. Some of the green bits had turned slightly brown, but nevertheless it still looked pretty revolting.

"Yuk," repeated Frances. She had voiced what I was thinking too, but I didn't say so. I got out my handkerchief and pretended to blow my nose.

"It's an old English delicacy," I said with muffled voice. She closed the grill and I returned the handkerchief to my pocket.

"If it was good enough for my forefathers, it's good enough for me," I said. "Why, they used to chop off men's ears for stealing hares."

"Well, all I can say is that I'm glad I've already had baked beans on toast," said Frances.

I grunted and went through to the sitting room to read the newspaper. I tried hard to concentrate, but it was difficult because the noxious smell pervaded the whole house. My stomach no longer rumbled with anticipation; instead it fluttered with that butterfly feeling which is well known to medical students who have had to take anatomy examinations.

Eventually the call came for me to go and eat and I went and sat down at the table in the small alcove just off the kitchen which we called 'the dining room'. I unfolded my napkin onto my knee and poured myself a glass of water. I took a gulp or two and it seemed to help. Frances came through from the kitchen with my plate held out at arm's length and unceremoniously plonked it down in front of me.

Somehow I had hoped that the cooking process would have made the meat look different. But it hadn't. It oozed slightly with gravy but it still looked green. Frances had put some mashed potatoes and sprouts on the plate as well, and the colour of the meat blended perfectly with that of the brussels.

I picked up my knife and fork. Then I put them down again. Suddenly I couldn't ignore the messages coming from my stomach any longer. I put my napkin to my mouth and rushed upstairs.

I always remember my professor of physiology telling us during a lecture one morning how he had vomited the night before. He hadn't vomited for twenty years or more, he said, but the old reflexes had still been there. The body has this built-in memory of how to do things. No man-made machine could ever hope to imitate its perfect ability to react automatically to given stimuli.

I thought of my professor of physiology as I vomited into the lavatory bowl. It was a lot less than twenty years since I had vomited. In fact the last occasion was after the annual Rugby Club Dinner. I had blamed the food but Frances had insisted that it had been due to something else. This time I knew the vomiting was due to food, but it was far worse than any alcoholic puke because it was psychologically induced. Wave after wave of nausea hit me as I thought of that revolting meat. I retched and retched and for a short time I thought that my end was nigh. But then the spasms began to die down and eventually I felt well enough to flush the lavatory and wash my face under the cold tap.

When I staggered downstairs again the flat smelled a lot sweeter. The windows had been opened and the hare had been consigned to the dustbin.

"I could have told you that would happen," said my wife triumphantly.

There are times in a marriage when it is best to remain silent and I judged that this was one of them.

19

"The trouble with you lot is that the people in real need never get to you. They're too frightened, for one thing. And not only that; for most of our customers you're too far away."

I was pontificating to my friend Charles in the Rugby Club bar. Charles had been at the dental school which was associated with my old teaching hospital and I had known him for several years. He had joined a dental group in Angleton at about the same time I had arrived in Tunford, and we had both been agreeably surprised when we had met up in the Rugby Club. He was a nice chap and he had a social conscience too. I could see that my remark had touched a bit of an exposed nerve.

"What do you mean, the people in need never reach us?" he asked.

"I mean what I say," I said. "Most of my customers with rotten teeth never go near a dentist until they have toothache. And even if I could persuade them to go for conservation work, your defences are too high. I know you are busy but the waiting time for appointments is ridiculous. What we really need is a dentist in the village, but there's not a hope in hell of that coming about, I know."

"Well, you're right about that," said Charles to the last point. There wasn't much hope of a young dentist striking out on his own in a place like Tunford. It would be too risky. There was far more security to be had as a member of one of the groups in the town.

"But tell you what," continued my friend, "if you see a filthy mouth which badly needs treatment, just give the patient a letter and send them to the surgery with something like 'Tunford Special' written on the outside of the envelope so my receptionist knows what's what. I guarantee I won't turn them away, and I will deal with them as soon as I can."

"Good man," I said. "You're on. Now what about another beer?"

The conversation progressed to less serious topics, but even though I drank quite a lot of beer during the course of that Saturday evening I didn't forget my friend's promise.

As it happened the very first patient to walk into my consulting room on Monday morning was Slopsey Finch, the poacher. Slopsey was a man and a half. Six feet two inches tall and nineteen stones in weight, he had spent most of his fifty years putting the fear of God into gamekeepers. But his reputation was far more fearsome than the man himself. I found him a polite, simple soul who was devoted to his old father, his guns and his ferrets, and I liked him. At least he was a real countryman, and I felt that he probably had more right to the occasional pheasant than did the rich businessmen who flocked to the local shoots from London.

"What's the trouble?" I asked.

He had taken his trilby hat off in respect for the doctor (a trait which endeared him to me. Some of our customers treated me like dirt).

"Oi got a tissic agin' Doctor," he said.

Slopsey suffered from recurrent bronchitis which was no doubt exacerbated by his nocturnal habits and his cigarette smoking, but no amount of nagging from me seemed to alter the pattern.

"Right, let's have a listen in then," I said, plugging my stethoscope into my ears.

Slopsey took off his jacket and Fair Isle pullover, undid one of the middle buttons of his shirt, and held the shirt apart at the level of the undone button to expose a small diamond shaped bit of flesh. His thick brown corduroy trousers were held up with an empty cartridge belt. A red and white spotted kerchief was wrapped round his neck, and the total effect was very piratical.

"OK. Turn your head to one side and take deep breaths in and out," I said. The huge bellows were put into operation and I moved my stethoscope over the tiny bit of exposed chest. I soon heard the expected squeaks.

But how shocked some of my teachers would have been to see me examine a chest in that way. It would have been no defence to say that Slopsey didn't like undressing and that when he did it was extremely time consuming. Only bad doctors examined chests like that. Well, bad doctor or no, at least I could now clear the average Tunford waiting room in double quick time, and that was more than most of my consultant teachers would have been capable of. In fact I would have liked to see them try it.

"Yes," I said to the patient. "You've got bronchitis again. I do wish you would stop smoking. How much phlegm are you coughing up?"

"Oh a fair bit."

"What colour is it?"

"Green. And it seems ter stick in me froat when Oi swaller."

"Let's have a look at your throat then," I said.

Slopsey obligingly opened his mouth and I depressed his tongue with a wooden spatula. His throat was a bit red, but the worst shock was his teeth. He only had about twelve stumps left but they were all black and exuded pus from around the sockets. As for the smell of his breath . . .

"Good God, man," I said. "Those teeth of yours are awful. When did you last see a dentist?"

"Oi think it was sometoime durin' the war," said Slopsey, looking sheepish.

"Well, you need to see one soon or you're going to have a lot of pain," I said. "Would you see a dentist friend of mine in Angleton if I fixed it up?"

"Yus, Oi reckon so," he replied with some courage. "But Oi don't think much o' they chaps."

I took out a pad of writing paper and scribbed a note to my friend Charles. I put it in an envelope and marked the outside

'TUNFORD SPECIAL' in large capital letters. Then I wrote out a prescription for some antibiotic and bronchodilator tablets for Slopsey's bronchitis. I handed over the results of my scribbling.

"Take this letter to the dentist when your bronchitis is better," I said. "The address is on the envelope. And there's no need to make an appointment first time. Just go along and make contact."

"Orl roight, Doc," said Slopsey resignedly. "Thankee." He had dressed again while I had been writing, so nothing kept him from disappearing from my consulting room as quickly as he could go.

*

To give the old boy credit he did exactly what I had advised him to do. He went along to Charles' surgery the very next market day, and the following Saturday my friend reported that he had seen my patient and recommended a full dental clearance. He also said there had been a full clearance of his waiting room when Slopsey had entered it. Apparently the townies hadn't taken too kindly to the appearance in their midst of a wild looking man from Tunford with a cartridge belt round his middle and a vicious looking dog at his heel.

"Soft lot," I commented. "But you will agree that he needed to see you," I said.

"Yes indeed," said Charles, who was obviously getting as much entertainment out of treating Slopsey as I did.

Slopsey lived up to our faith in him. Over the next few weeks his mouth was cleaned up bit by bit. He couldn't face a general anaesthetic and so Charles removed his teeth for him in three bloody sessions. His mouth healed up nicely and he went to have an impression taken for false teeth. The weeks passed and then he had an invitation to go and see the dentist to collect the new teeth.

He was delighted with them. He put them in and could hardly believe it when he looked at himself in the mirror. This was a new image altogether. He smiled down at his dog and the animal whimpered in disbelief.

"Thank yew very much," said Slopsey.

Charles was really pleased. He had a warm do-gooding glow inside him which made him feel really great, and he was almost sorry when Slopsey said he had to go. But go he had to. He left the dental surgery and stepped outside. The street was very busy with a constant stream of traffic and the poacher had to wait at the kerb before he could cross. As he waited he had a tickle in his nose. He rubbed his nose but it did no good. The urge to sneeze became irresistible. He could contain it no more.

"AAAAtishooo," he went, and the beautiful, precious new teeth were ejected from Slopsey's mouth and into the roadway like a pip from an orange. They lay there undamaged for an instant, but before he could rescue them they were smashed to smithereens by the wheels of a passing sugar beet wagon.

When you are a poacher you have to be philosophical. Slopsey didn't weep or stamp his feet. All he did was utter a few well chosen expletives, and then he crossed the road and went straight into the Red Lion to drown his sorrows.

He never went back to Charles for another set of teeth. Looks or no looks he couldn't go through all that again.

149

20

"I think you've had a heart attack," I said as I straightened up.

"Are ye sure it's not just indigestion?" asked the Irishman from his bed.

"Well, no. I can't be absolutely sure. But that pain going down your left arm sounds very suspicious. I think I had better get you into hospital to have some tests done."

"Hospital? Oi never taut ye'd be sendin' me there. The pain's nearly gone now. Are ye sure it's necessary?"

"Yes," I said. "We need to get an accurate diagnosis in the first place. And if you have had a coronary you should be nursed in bed for a while. There's nobody to do that here is there now?"

"That's true," he replied. "Ah well, anythin' you say, Doc."

I liked Patrick Molloy. He was a labourer with a civil engineering firm and he had lived in his caravan in Tunford for the past three years. He was a bachelor and his wants seemed to be few. Somewhere to lay his head, cigarettes unlimited, a few pints of beer in his belly every night and he seemed to be happy. I wondered how long it had been since he had been to Ireland. His accent with its lilting, musical quality which was a pleasant change from the East Anglian rasp, sounded as if he had left only yesterday.

Mrs. Pleasance at Poplar Farm had telephoned for me just half an hour before. Patrick's caravan was parked in a meadow at the back of the farm and she had had the message from the milkman that the Irishman was ill. I hadn't been too pleased to be called. It was just before morning surgery and I had barely had time to read the post. But you can't put off a visit to a potential case of coronary thrombosis, and now I was there I was glad I had come straightaway.

"Right," I said. "I'll nip across to the farm and 'phone the Angleton General. I'll be back in a minute."

I stepped out of the caravan. It wasn't raining now, but it had done overnight. The ground was saturated. The row of tall poplar trees at the back of the farm swayed in the wind and the sky was uniformly grey. Often you could stop and look in wonder at these East Anglian skies. The vast multicoloured panorama created by sun, sky and clouds was at times a thing of beauty. But today there was no free show. Today the sky could have belonged to industrial Lancashire.

I had driven my car right up to the side of Patrick's caravan, but it didn't seem worth getting in it to go to the farmhouse. I was thankful I had my gumboots on. They were now as essential a part of the equipment in the boot as the shovel and I had slipped into them before I had started out. I had expected it to be wet and I hadn't been disappointed. I sloshed across the meadow, through the gate and between the buildings in the stack yard. There wasn't a farm animal in sight. Like a lot of East Anglian farms, Poplar Farm was completely arable. The Pleasances had a cat, and that was about all. The buildings merely housed rows and rows of field implements, tractors and sacks of fertiliser.

I reached the back door of the farmhouse and knocked upon it lightly. Mrs. Pleasance answered.

"Oh hello," I said. "I wonder if I could possibly use your telephone, please?"

Mrs. Pleasance lived up to her name. She was a pleasant, middle-aged lady who had once been a teacher.

"Certainly, Doctor," she said. "How is Patrick?"

"I'm afraid the milkman's suspicions may have been correct," I said. "It sounds as if he could have had a small coronary. Anyway, I'm sending him into hospital."

"Poor chap. Can I help at all?"

"Only by letting me use your 'phone," I said.

"Of course, I didn't mean to delay you," she said. "Come in. It's through the hall."

151

I went through and fixed up the admission with the house-man at the hospital. Then I telephoned the ambulance control and gave them careful instructions how to get to Poplar Farm. I went back into the kitchen.

"Thank you very much," I said. "The ambulance should be along in a few minutes. It might help if you could keep a look out for it."

"I will," she said. "Poor Patrick, I do hope he will be all right. He's a funny one, you know, but my husband and I are quite attached to him. He pays his rent on the dot and he's as good a tenant as you could wish."

"I expect he'll be all right in a few weeks, even if he has had a coronary," I said. "Anyway, I had better get back to him now. Thanks again for the use of your 'phone."

"You're welcome, any time," she said.

I left the farmhouse and tracked back to the caravan. Patrick was still lying as I had left him and he seemed pretty chirpy.

"That's that," I said. "The ambulance won't be long. How d'you feel?"

"Foine," he said. "Oi've no pain at all now. Oi reckon Oi'll be wastin' ivverybody's toime."

"No, I don't think so," I said.

I sat down on the edge of his bunk and penned a letter to the house physician at the hospital. I put it in an envelope and left it on the small bedside table. Then I looked at my watch.

"Goodness," I said. "Surgery started fifteen minutes ago. I'll have to move. You should be all right on your own till the ambulance comes. Just stay where you are."

I snapped my bag shut.

"Best of luck," I said.

"Tanks," replied Patrick, and I stepped outside again. I hated being late for surgery. It always threw the whole day into turmoil. The waiting room got very full, the patients got more and more stroppy, and you had to work feverishly against the clock to try and catch up.

I got into the car and started the engine. I selected first gear and let out the clutch. The car went forwards a few inches and then slowly came to a halt with the back wheels spinning round uselessly in the mire. I stepped on the accelerator but nothing happened.

'That's all I bloody well need,' I thought. 'A waiting room full of patients and I'm stuck here in the mud.' I put the engine into neutral and got out of the vehicle. The place where I had parked was about the wettest in the meadow. When I had first arrived I had swung the car round so that it was facing the gate again, and in doing that I had driven off the rutted track which led to the farmyard. This track had been strengthened at some time or another with stones and rubble and its surface was relatively sound. The only hope for me of getting out of the meadow was to regain the track, which was only a few feet over to my left.

I stepped back into the car again. The back wheels had dug themselves into the mud pretty successfully, but when I engaged reverse gear, let out the clutch and stepped hard on the accelerator, I slowly managed to unstick them. When I was on firmer ground, I paused before engaging first gear again. Then I turned the steering wheel hard down to the left and charged forwards. The car lurched ahead. At one point I very nearly got stuck, but this time the vehicle seemed to have hidden resources of power. I sailed through the mud and onto the track. I gave a little cheer, but it was only when I happened to glance in my driving mirror that I realised why I had been so successful. My newly diagnosed case of coronary thrombosis, Patrick Molloy, had been pushing with all his might from the rear.

21

"I'll have the last waltz with you . . .
Two lonely people together . . ."

. . . Crooned the singer. We held each other tightly as we
danced. It was the annual Rugby Club Ball in Angleton's Corn
Exchange. The evening had gone very well indeed and both
Frances and I had enjoyed it. We didn't get the chance for much
night life in Tunford, and even if we had had the opportunity to
go out more often, in the last few weeks we wouldn't have been
able to do so anyway, because Frances had been feeling pretty
rotten with the sickness of early pregnancy. But now that she
was about seventeen weeks gone, she felt a lot better and she
looked a picture of health. Her skin and hair had taken on a
new lustre and she was absolutely blooming. I thought how
lucky I was to be married to such a girl. Sometimes I had envied
Timothy Bacon and his freedom from matrimonial ties but his
wasn't an enviable state really. I was quite happy to be an old
married man, especially now.

There was a roll on the drums, the lights went up and the
band launched into 'God Save the Queen'. We stood until they
had finished.

"That's it folks," said the singer over the microphone.
"See you again next year, I hope. Mind how you drive on the
way home."

We gave him a clap.

"There, he says you've got to drive home," I said to my
wife. "Do you feel up to it?"

"Better than you, I've no doubt," she laughed.

It was true. I had been pretty free with the right elbow, and
there was little doubt that my reflexes wouldn't be as good as

my wife's. And if the police stopped the car with me at the wheel, I doubt if they would have been as lenient with me as the local bobby had been with Timothy's grandfather. It was a tale my partner often told. His grandfather had been driving home from a dinner not long after the 1914—18 War when he had knocked the local policeman off his bicycle. The policeman had climbed out of the ditch, saluted and said, "Very sorry to be in your way, Doctor."

But times had changed since then. I handed Frances the car keys and we went over to our table to say goodbye to our group of friends. My wife collected her handbag and we moved towards the exit via the cloakroom. It didn't take long before we were in the street. Outside the pavement was wet with rain and there was still a light drizzle falling. Our car was parked in the square about fifty yards from the Corn Exchange but we managed to reach it without getting too wet. In no time at all we were spinning along the main Tunford road and we reached the village about twenty five minutes after leaving the town.

Harry Bailey's eldest daughter Susan had been babysitting for us and she got up sleepily from an armchair as we walked into the sitting room of the flat.

"Everything quiet, Susan?" asked Frances.

"Yes. Not a squeak," she replied.

"Well, thank you very much," said Frances as she searched in her handbag for the usual fee. "I'm sorry we're so late."

"Oh, that's all right," said Susan. "Thanks," she added as she took the money. "I didn't expect you home early. And anyway it's mock A levels for the science sixth tomorrow. Being a linguist, I don't have to go to school."

"That's good," said Frances.

We said goodnight and Frances showed Susan to the door. One of the advantages of living in the middle of the village like we did, was that we didn't have to ferry the babysitter home. Susan only had to take a few steps to her own door just down the street. I heard Frances shutting the door behind the girl and then she came back into the sitting room.

"Would you like coffee?" she asked.

"No thanks," I said. "My head's going round a bit and it says it wants to be put on the pillow."

"You shouldn't drink so much," she said.

"I know that," I replied. "But the trouble is that I always get carried away by the company. I wasn't as bad as Tony Mossman anyway."

"That's true," she agreed.

I turned off the light in the sitting room and we went upstairs. Frances popped into Sally's room to check on the sleeping infant, while I went into the bathroom to brush my teeth.

I was in bed and nearly asleep by the time my wife joined me only a few minutes later. The romantic feeling I had had when we were dancing had long worn off, and there was no danger of me claiming my conjugal rights on this night. That's what alcohol does for you. Frances snuggled into my back and I was in the land of nod before you could say Angleton Rugby Club. But my bliss was short lived. I must have been asleep for about an hour when the telephone rang raucously and insistently in my left ear.

"Oh no," I mumbled as I regained consciousness. I switched on the light and picked up the receiver.

"Dr. Slater," I croaked.

"That's moi woife," said a voice. "Can yew come roight away? The baby's nearly here."

"Who's that speaking?"

"Fred Deacon."

My mind slowly focussed. Cynthia Deacon was expecting her third child. The first had been a difficult forceps delivery, and the second had arrived by Caesarian section. When she had come to see me early in this pregnancy I had referred her to Hector MacDonald and she was booked for hospital delivery.

"But she's due to have it in hospital, isn't she?" I said. "Why are you ringing me?"

"That's too late. Oi'd never get her there. Can yew come quick." He sounded very agitated.

Technically, of course, I was off duty, but Timothy and I had a gentleman's agreement that we would attend all our own maternity cases. It made sense, because there was little point in giving a woman six or seven months of personal ante-natal care, establishing a relationship, and then deserting her in her hour of need. And another good reason for our system was that deliveries often took quite a long time. It was better for the rest of the practice if the doctor attended them when he was off duty, because he could then give his undivided attention to the case and leave the colleague on duty free to deal with the general emergencies.

"OK, I'm coming," I said. "Can you give the midwife a ring too?"

I put the receiver down and got out of bed. It was only when I stood up that I realised how awful I felt. The euphoria of the alcohol had worn off and I was left feeling very giddy. I had the mother and father of all headaches, my mouth felt like the crater of a burnt-out volcano and my teeth, despite the use of the toothbrush before I had gone to bed, were already coated with an unpleasant tasting scum. I was really in no state to go delivering babies. No doubt if I had been a lorry driver there would have been a law to say that I had exceeded my mileage. But there's no similar law which says that doctors must stop work no matter how little sleep they have had or how rotten they feel.

The telephone bell had wakened Frances too.

"Why have you got to go out?" she asked. "I thought you were off duty."

"It's a ruddy midder case," I said. "Just my luck."

"Poor you," she said. "Are you sober enough?"

"I think so," I lied.

157

It was poor me indeed. By this time I had nearly dressed again. The nearest clothes to hand had been my dress shirt and my dinner jacket, and that's what I had put on. At least it would advertise to all concerned that I was really off duty.

"You had better go to sleep anyway," I said as I switched off the light.

"I doubt if I will," she said.

"Well, it's not far and with a bit of luck I won't be long," I said. I felt my way to the upstairs landing. The sense of urgency was slowly conquering the alcohol and my system was gradually getting into overdrive. I stumbled down the stairs wondering what awful obstetric complications Mrs. Deacon was going to produce this time. A ruptured uterus, perhaps? It wasn't at all impossible with her previous history of a Caesarian section.

'God,' I prayed. 'Let it not be anything terrible. This poor drunken frame just couldn't cope.' I threw on my overcoat and opened the front door. A cold blast of air hit me in the face and I shuddered. What a life; it wasn't worth it if they had paid us five times the money.

The car engine started easily, and in no time at all I was pulling up outside the Deacons' house, which was only half a mile outside the village. Mr. Deacon was a smallholder and he and his family lived in a small bungalow surrounded by mud and pig pens. I think it was a precarious living. When pig prices were up he did reasonably well, but when feed prices went up too, he barely made a living. Unlike the big boys he just couldn't switch to something else or even help out on costs by producing some of his own pig food. It seemed to be hard and grinding work and was far from being a rural idyll.

I left my car in the road, grabbed my midder bag from the boot and squelched my way to the house. There had been no time to think of gum boots and I quickly found that my dress shoes weren't waterproof. The back door was open and I walked right in. The dog was shut in a back room but it started howling and scraping at the door when it heard me. I was glad it was locked up. I didn't fancy coping with the hound of the Baskervilles as well as everything else. The two children were in a back bedroom. They too had sensed that something was amiss and both were crying. The general atmosphere was one of pandemonium and Mr. Deacon didn't look as if he was coping too well. He was in a complete dither.

"Thank God yew've come, Doctor," he said as soon as he clapped eyes on me. "Oi think yew're just in toime."

I followed him through to a front bedroom. His wife was lying on top of the bed in her nightdress. She looked to be in agony.

"Hello, Doctor," she squeezed out between clenched teeth. "Oi'm afraid it's too late for the hospital."

"Yes, it looks like it," I replied with a tight little laugh.

"Oh, oh, here it comes," she said, and before I had time to blink, the baby's head appeared. I threw off my overcoat.

"Go and get me a bowl of hot water and some newspapers," I said to the husband, and as I did so I went on my knees and attempted to assist the delivery. There was no time to wash my hands or even open my midder bag. It was all a tremendous fumble, but the baby seemed to come easily enough. It was a good sized boy and he cried immediately.

"It's a boy," I said.

"Oh, not another," said Mrs. Deacon. Her pain had gone.

I looked around. Nothing had been prepared because Mrs. Deacon had expected to have the baby in hospital. Instead, she had delivered him onto her own sheets and there was blood and amniotic fluid everywhere. I went for my instruments in my bag and went through my usual routine of sucking out the baby's nasal passages and dividing the umbilical cord. I handed the child straight to his delighted mother.

Mr. Deacon came back with a large plastic washing-up bowl half full with hot water, some soap and some old newspapers.

"It's a boy," I told him.

He grinned.

159

"Well done," he said to his wife. "Oi thought it would be."
He looked admiringly at his new son.

"He's got a foine pair of lungs, hain't he, Doctor?"

"Yes there's nothing much wrong there," I replied. "Now
can you get me a pudding bowl and make a cup of tea while I
deliver the afterbirth," I asked.

He soon came back with the pudding bowl and then went
off to brew up. I suppose Mr. Deacon must have seen thousands
of pig farrowings and he was unlikely to be upset by the sight of
a placenta being delivered, but I preferred him to be out of the
way just in case something went wrong. I washed my hands,
placed some of the old newspapers between Mrs. Deacon's legs,
and a few minutes later delivered the placenta into the pudding
basin, with minimal blood loss.

"Good," I said. "Everything's gone very well, but it looks as
if there's quite a tear in your tail, I'm afraid. I'm going to have
to put in a few stitches."

She nodded and I stood up again for the first time since I had
entered the room. There was no hurry now and the anxiety was
over, but as I stood up I felt sick and giddy. I suddenly became
very aware of the warm nauseating smell of the blood and amniotic
fluid. Some of the blood had found its way on to the sleeve of my
dinner jacket, and when I put my hand to my brow I got a concentrated whiff of it. I sat down on the bed and supported my
reeling head in my hands. It was the closest to fainting I had ever
been; when I was a student I had always regarded those people
who passed out when they watched operations as cissies who
were only fit to be psychiatrists. For years now blood and gore
had been part of my life and it shouldn't have upset me. But
just at that moment it was upsetting me very much.

"Are yew orl roight, Doctor?" asked Mrs. Deacon.

"Yes, I think it's just the lack of sleep," I lied. "I've been
out of bed quite a lot recently." I didn't mention the alcohol.

"And you've been out too?" she said, alluding to my dinner
jacket for the first time. "Yew were off duty, Oi suppose?"

"Yes," I said.

"Who'd be a doctor," she said, sympathetically.

I felt quite guilty. A few moments ago Mrs. Deacon's life could have been in danger, and now she was busy being sorry for me. I didn't deserve it at all because it was my own silly fault I had drunk too much. But just at that moment Nurse Parmenter walked in. Whatever my feelings about Nurse Parmenter had been in the past I had never been so glad to see her. Had I not felt so ill I might even have embraced her. It was the relief of Mafeking all over again.

She took in the situation at a glance.

"How about a cup of tea for everyone," she suggested, predictably.

"It's on its way," I said.

"Do you feel all right, Doctor," she asked.

"I'm coming round," I said. "But I would be very grateful if you could take my instruments into the kitchen and give them a boil. Mrs. Deacon's going to need a few stitches, I'm afraid."

I kept my suturing instruments in a long stainless steel box which was designed for the purpose. The idea was that before you used the instruments you covered them with water and then put the container on a cooker to boil the water and sterilise everything in the box. Nurse Parmenter took the whole lot off to the kitchen. Then she came back and bustled round tidying up. The tea came. Mrs. Deacon and I sipped ours but I was surprised to see that Nurse Parmenter left hers until everything was reasonably ship-shape. In particular she made a great to-do about wrapping up the baby and placing him in a cot which Mr. Deacon had produced from a back room somewhere.

I don't normally like sugar in tea but Mr. Deacon had laced mine with about three teaspoonsful. I didn't complain. The hot sweet fluid seemed to have a reviving effect and the swimminess slowly left me.

Nurse Parmenter came back with the instruments. She had drained the boiling water off in the kitchen, and when they had

161

cooled down they would be ready to use. She changed the hot water in the plastic bowl which Mr. Deacon had left on the dresser and after a few minutes I was able to wash my hands, put on a plastic apron, some sterile rubber gloves, and set about repairing Cynthia Deacon's tail. It was a job I had been used to for several years now. When we were students the obstetric housemen had been very keen to teach us how to 'sew up'. A set of competent students were worth their weight in gold because they often saved the houseman from getting out of bed. But whoever did it, in all the establishments in which I had worked it was always insisted that the women were sewn up immediately. I had heard stories about certain hospitals where the women who delivered at night were left unsutured until the morning. If this was true I thought it was very cruel. I certainly wouldn't have let that happen to my wife, and I didn't think it should happen to anybody else's wife either.

I must have done the operation scores of times by now and I could almost have done it blindfolded. First a continuous cat-gut suture starting at the apex of the tear. Then some deep interrupted sutures to bring in the muscle layers followed by some interrupted silk sutures to the skin. Finally, expel the blood clot from the vagina and put your finger in the rectum to check that none of the sutures had penetrated the back passage. It could be constipating if they had.

Of course, it was all very easy in hospital with lots of nurses to help, the patient's legs up in stirrups, and a good operating light. But in general practice it was a lot harder. You usually had to do it with the patient lying on a low saggy bed with the light being provided by the midwife holding a torch — the 'spotlight on charm' as we always joked.

Mrs. Parmenter had her torch with her and I got her to stand at the foot of the bed and shine it at the area in question while I put the local anaesthetic in with a large syringe.

I waited a short time for the anaesthetic to work and then

set about my task. My giddiness seemed to have gone completely, and I did what I thought was a very creditable job.

"There," I said as I put in the last stitch. "You're as good as new now. Nurse will take the stitches out on about the tenth day."

"Thanks, Doctor," said the patient as I completed the job. She was grateful I had finished as they always were. Although I had achieved adequate local anaesthesia, like most other women Mrs. Deacon probably felt that having the stitches put in was worse than having the baby. I could understand it. The procedure was pretty undignified.

The midwife put a pad on the patient's perineum and I helped her fold a clean sheet under Mrs. Deacon. Then I retreated to the kitchen to wash my bloodied instruments. The dog started barking and scratching again as I went down the passage.

"Shut up," shouted Mr. Deacon at the animal. He was still installed in the kitchen and the air was heavy with cigarette smoke. The two toddlers, both of them quiet now, were with him.

"You can take them through to see their brother," I said. "It looks as if you've got yet another pig farmer."

"He laughed. "Yes, Oi don't know how Oi'm goin' ter set 'em all up," he said with mock concern. He took the children through to see the baby as I had suggested and I set about washing my instruments. When I had done so I dried them carefully with a clean tea towel and replaced them in the stainless steel box which I had also washed and dried.

I went back into the bedroom. Everything was spick and span.

I examined the baby to check for congenital abnormalities. There didn't seem to be any.

"He's a fine specimen," I said to Mrs. Deacon.

"Is the uterus well contracted, Nurse?"

"Yes."

"And the blood pressure?"

"One twenty over eighty."

"Good," I said. "I'll be off then. See you later this morning Mrs. Deacon. And thank you very much indeed Mrs. Parmenter."

The nurse nodded. I packed my midder bag, found my overcoat, put it on, said goodbye to everyone and left the house. I felt fine now. As I splashed my way back to the car I didn't give a thought for my dress suit. It was covered in mud, blood and amniotic fluid, but I didn't give a damn. I was tired but happy — elated even. I had really got away with it. When I thought of the disasters which could have befallen Mrs. Deacon I realised that I was very lucky indeed to have such a happy outcome from the night's work. Nobody in his right mind would book a woman who had had a previous Caesarian section for home confinement. All the books were quite adamant on the subject. But by the perverse laws of Nature, Mrs. Deacon had had a far more normal birth at home than she had ever had in hospital. It had been nothing to do with me, of course, but I had been there, and despite the fact that I had done little more than put in a few stitches, I felt strangely satisfied with myself.

When I got home the clock stood at five to four. Frances was asleep, and I managed to undress and get into bed without waking her. It didn't take me long to drop off and it seemed only a moment later that it was seven thirty and the alarm clock was ringing. Frances got up, but I just groaned and rolled over. In a few minutes she came back into the room with a cup of tea.

"Just what I needed," I said. "I think I'm getting more like Nurse Parmenter every day." I told her the story of the night's happenings and she was amused.

"What did they call the baby?" she asked when I had finished.

"I don't know," I said. "There was too much going on to ask questions like that."

Frances seemed disappointed.

I drank the tea and went to have a bath and shave. Then I

had breakfast and at five minutes to nine I walked into the dispensary. Timothy was in there talking to Mr. Somerville.

"Oh hello," he said, taking in my pallid look with an understanding glance. "How was the Rugger Ball?"

I told him.

22

The spring sunshine shone on his face and for the first time I noticed how pale he looked.

"Are you feeling all right?" I asked.

"Yes," he replied. "Just a bit breathless, chancetoime."

"Well, it looks as if you're anaemic to me," I said. "Let's go into the house again and I'll have a look at you. I'll just get my bag from my car."

He waited for me at the door and then I followed him back into the house with my bag in my hand.

I loved this old place. Until five years before it had been Tunford's bakery and Frank had been the baker. The shop was laid out just as it had been on the day trading had stopped. There was a simple wooden counter set on the brick floor, a high wooden desk, and at the back a huge brick oven with a cast iron door. The oven was recessed into the wall for twelve or thirteen feet and when it was in operation the whole house must have been as warm as toast. Hung up on the wall of the shop were two long paddle shaped tools called peelers which had been used to put the dough into the oven.

I don't think Frank could bear to change anything, and in fact I think he had a sneaking thought that one day he might start baking again, that is, if his wife would let him. Quite rightly, he argued that he hadn't had an illness since he had had tonsillitis in Salonika during the First World War, but his wife was probably equally right when she insisted that it wasn't a good thing for a man in his seventies to be getting up at four o'clock every morning to set about baking bread.

Mrs. Whiting had won the battle over retirement, but she had agreed with Frank that the best thing to do was to just shut the shop and not sell up and move away, which seems to be the pattern for so many folk who retire. It was far better for them to continue to live in the place where they had spent their working lives and where everyone knew and respected them.

And I don't think Frank could have lived anywhere else but in Tunford. In his eyes Tunford was the only place where a body could possibly be happy. Whitings had been buried in the churchyard for centuries and he felt that he was as much a part of the local scenery as the trees around the village pump. His whole life, apart from his war service, had been spent in the bakery. His father had owned Tunford's windmill and Frank had moved into the bakery as soon as he had married. When his father had died he had inherited the mill and run it as a working concern until it had been blown down in a storm during the nineteen fifties.

The bakery was only a very short distance from the surgery flat and our acquaintance had started with the nod of neighbours. But soon I was having lengthy chats with him, and now I was in the habit of dropping into see my friend whenever the practice was slack. Frank didn't seem like a man of seventy eight at all. He was nearly fifty years my senior and yet it sometimes seemed that we were both still boys. He had a very lively mind and had been interested in sport all his life. Frank had been a soccer man, of course, but nevertheless he listened intently to my accounts of the doings of the Angleton Third Fifteen. In my turn I was fascinated by stories of trimming the sails of a post mill in winter gales, of the First World War and of Tunford's cricket team of fifty years before. Some of the heroes of the cricketing stories were still about. Arty, Nicker, Dido and Jock; I knew them as little old men, but learning about their past exploits somehow seemed to give them a fresh vigour when I met them in the street or surgery.

Just this morning I had had another fascinating chat about Tunford's past. It was Saturday and Frank and I had each had a pre-lunch beer together. He had been seeing me out of his front door when I had noticed how pale he was. As a matter of fact Frances had mentioned to me about three weeks before that my old friend had seemed to be puffing a lot when she had seen him riding up the street on his bicycle. But I had pooh poohed her.

"He is seventy eight," I had pointed out. But as Frank's doctor I had been doing him a disservice by seeing him so often. It is a well known fact in general practice that the more often you see your patients, the less likely you are to notice gradual changes in them. The classical missed condition is myxoedema, where the regular GP fails to note that the patient's voice is getting more hoarse, her hair more coarse and her skin very dry. It is usually left to one of the doctor's partners to make the diagnosis when the 'proper doctor' is on holiday.

Mrs. Whiting came out of the sitting room as we re-entered the house. She was about ten years younger than her husband and I liked her almost as much as I did him. Both the Whitings were unpretentious folk with roots deep in the soil of East Anglia.

"I'm sorry, Mrs. Whiting," I said. "I know it's nearly lunchtime but I just noticed how pale Mr. Whiting is, and I thought I had better have a look at him."

"Well, Oi'd be very pleased, Doctor," she replied. "Oi've been worried about him for some toime, but he kept sayin' he was orl roight."

"Perhaps you could go upstairs, get undressed and get into bed, Mr. Whiting," I said. Despite our friendship we still called each other 'Mr.' and 'Dr.' respectively. It just seemed more natural that way.

"Whatever yew say," said Frank. "But Oi don't know what all the fuss is about. Oi feel OK."

"Well, just yew do as the Doctor says," said Mrs. Whiting.

He went upstairs and I followed him into the bedroom. As he undressed I noticed how breathless he was. Climbing the stairs and the effort of taking off his clothes were almost too much for him. His skin was as pale as the loaves he once baked and his ear lobes were nearly transparent. How blind I had been not to see it all before.

"How long have you been getting as breathless as this?" I asked when he finally lay down on the bed. He had removed all his clothes but his underpants.

"Oh, a month or two."

"Why didn't you tell me?"

"Oi thought it was moi age."

"Had any indigestion?"

"No."

"How's your appetite?"

"That's never been better."

"Bowels OK?"

"Yes. Regular as clockwork."

"The motions haven't been black, have they?"

"No."

"And the waterworks. They OK?"

"Yes."

"No blood in the urine?"

"No."

"Well, just lie back and let's have a look at you shall we?"

I examined him thoroughly, but when I had finished I was none the wiser than when I had started. Apart from the extreme pallor there was nothing abnormal to find. Even his blood pressure was that of a young man.

"You certainly look anaemic, but I can't explain why," I said. "If it's all right by you, I'll take a specimen of blood and send it off to the hospital."

"Roight yew are," said Frank, philosophically.

I partially reinflated the cuff of the blood pressure machine. A nice fat vein stood up in the cubital fossa, and I had soon taken about four cubic centimetres of blood with a plastic syringe and transferred it to one of the little sequestrine bottles we used for sending specimens to the hospital. I carefully labelled the bottle, and then put it together with a request form in a large brown envelope addressed to the Consultant Pathologist at the Angleton Hospital.

"OK," I said, as I removed the deflated arm cuff and repacked my bag. "Just take it easy for a day or two until we get the result from the hospital."

"Can Oi get dressed now?" he asked.

"Certainly," I said. "Carry on as normally as possible, although it might be wise if you kept off your bike. I think it is just an anaemia, and we should be able to put you right in due course. But we will have to find out what sort of anaemia it is before you can have any treatment."

"Oi understand," he said.

"Right then. I'll be off for lunch," I said. "I'm sorry to have delayed yours."

"That's orl roight," he said. "Thank yew for the trouble yew've taken."

I went downstairs again and met Mrs. Whiting at the bottom of the flight.

"He certainly is very anaemic," I said, "But I don't know why. The most likely thing, I suppose, is pernicious anaemia. That's due to a shortage of vitamin B12 and we can easily cure it with some injections. Let's hope it is that and nothing else. I've taken some blood from him, by the way, but I can't do anything else until I hear from the hospital."

"Well, thank you for what yew've done, Doctor," said Mrs. Whiting. "Oi really do appreciate it."

It was the old old story. I was thanked when I had done nothing. You could even say that I had been negligent.

"It's nothing," I said. "I'm sorry that I didn't notice he was going behind a bit sooner. I see him often enough don't I?"

"That yew do," she said with a little laugh.

As I left the bakery this time I shut the double 'stable' type door behind me myself. The door suddenly took on a new significance. In Frank Whiting's case I might be accused of shutting the stable door after the horse had bolted. I hoped not.

On the way past the post office I dropped the brown envelope in the box. It would arrive at the hospital on Monday.

Frances wondered why I was late for lunch so I told her what had been happening.

"You were right about Frank," I said. "He is very breathless, and it's because he's anaemic."

"I thought there was something wrong," replied my wife.

"Well, I hope it's nothing more serious than pernicious anaemia," I said. "If he's got something like a carcinoma of the caecum, he won't take too kindly to going into hospital for an operation. I feel a right Charlie seeing him so often and yet missing something so obvious. But they say it happens to all GPs sometime or another."

"I suppose so," said Frances. "Was Mrs. Whiting very upset?"

"Not very," I said. "Like Frank, she has a faith in Dr. Slater which I find very chilling."

Just after surgery on Monday morning the pathologist from the hospital telephoned me.

"You know that specimen of blood you sent in from a Frank Whiting," he said.

"Oh yes," I replied, and then briefly outlined the story.

"Well, his haemoglobin is only three point eight grams," he said. I whistled.

"Goodness me," I said. "No wonder he was breathless when he rode his bike."

As a matter of fact people usually start getting some sort of symptoms when their haemoglobin falls below ten grams. Three point eight grams, I had been taught, was only just about compatible with life.

"Yes," said the pathologist. "Well, I think the best thing would be for him to come into hospital. We need to do some more blood tests and perhaps a bone marrow too. You know it would be useful if you chaps could send us a smear of blood on a slide when you send in your requests. The sequestrine plays hell with the cells."

"Sorry," I said. "I keep forgetting to put some microscope slides in my bag. But thanks anyway."

"Not at all," he said. "It looks an interesting one this. I shouldn't be surprised if it turns out to be something funny."

"It's not pernicious anaemia then?"

"No, I don't think so."

"Well, thanks for 'phoning," I said. "He's not going to be too keen to come in but I'll go and try to persuade him."

We said goodbye and I put the receiver down. I hot footed it to the bakery as soon as I could. As I had expected Frank was extremely reluctant to go into hospital, but eventually I persuaded him that that would be the best course.

A few days later we knew the worst. He had sideroblastic anaemia, a very rare form of anaemia for which there is really no cure. The hospital doctors did their best. They tried him on various drugs, but when these failed, they gave him a blood transfusion just to make him feel better. He returned to Tunford for a few weeks but then in the end I had to send him back again.

I visited him in hospital, but although he was glad to see me he was a shadow of his former self and he died a few days later.

I was very upset and the hospital doctors wondered why. After all it was only a seventy eight year old man who had come to the end of his natural span, so why all the fuss? But to me that old man had been a real friend, and the only thing I could comfort myself with was that if I had made the diagnosis sooner it would have made little difference. Nevertheless, I had learned my lesson. From now on, if ever I became very friendly with a patient I would ask Timothy to take over as the doctor. It would be much the safest thing to do for all concerned.

23

Instinctively, I knew that the knock on the door was for me, even though I wasn't in my own house. It had an urgency about it which you wouldn't somehow expect from the everyday callers at Mrs. Byrne's.

"All right, I'll answer it," I said, getting up and putting down my cup and saucer on the table. My visits to Granny Byrne had become almost purely social. True, the old girl did have a bit of heart failure which required a certain amount of medication, but I certainly didn't need to call on her every month as I did. We did a lot of this sort of social visiting; too much in my opinion. The real reason why I called was that the old lady was lonely. I didn't mind having a cup of tea and a chat with her, but it really was a waste of my professional time. And unlike my old friend Frank Whiting, Granny Byrne was a bit of a bore. No doubt Dr. Long had sucked up to the Byrnes because Mr. Byrne had been the village butcher before he had died. Prior to the NHS most tradesmen had paid their doctor's bills promptly, and there would probably have been a brace or two of pheasants at Christmas too. I resented having to practise the way Dr. Long had done but the trouble was it was difficult to break the habits of centuries. If I didn't call every month, Mrs. Byrne's name would appear in the practice's visiting book on a day when I was otherwise very busy indeed.

I strode out into the hall. There was a strong smell of polish. The grandfather clock and an ancient oak chest gleamed with a patina you couldn't reproduce. Mrs. Byrne's daily help still put hours every week into polishing the furniture, and the same service had obviously been performed by countless hands before hers.

I opened the door. A scruffy looking boy of about ten was standing there. 'Simon Page' I thought correctly.

"Me Mum says, can yew come quick," he said. "The bus has run over me brother."

"Goodness me," I said. "Why yes, I'll come."

I looked up the street. The school bus had just disgorged its contents only forty yards away. There was a whole gaggle of mothers and children near the back of the vehicle and there appeared to be a lot of excitement. A child was lying on the pavement and one of the women was making a noise like an Arab lady at a sheik's funeral. It looked bad.

My heart started away on its familiar pat-a-pat.

"I'll just get my bag, I said, "and then I'll be with you."

I dashed back into Granny Byrne's sitting room.

"There's been an accident," I said. "I've got to go. See you next month." I picked up my bag and flew.

They say it's unprofessional to run, but I covered those forty yards from the front door to the back of the bus like an Olympic sprinter. Hang the dignity, a child's life was at stake.

"What happened?" I asked as I fought my way through the scrum. Mrs. Page was using all her energy with the screaming. She didn't even stop to answer my question.

"The bus went over the pavement as it turned round," somebody else answered. John Page was lying on the pavement. I knew him well. The Pages were frequent attenders at the surgery.

Although the boy was lying down, he was still conscious and still breathing normally. There didn't seem to be any blood about either. I knelt down beside him.

"Where does it hurt?" I asked.

"It's me foot, Doctor," he replied, as though he was in some pain.

"You mean the bus ran over your foot?"

"Yes, that 'un," he said, pointing to the right one.

I took off his right shoe and sock as gently as I could. Ankle movements were full and all the tarsal and metatarsal bones seemed to be intact. I hadn't got X-ray eyes, of course, but I was pretty sure there was no serious damage. The only demonstrable injury was a bit of bruising on the very tip of his right big toe. He had had a very lucky escape. If the bus had really run over his foot it would have mangled it.

"He's all right, Mrs. Page," I said as I straightened up. "He's not badly hurt at all. Just a bruised toe."

But the wailing continued. She really had worked herself up into a frenzy.

"He's all right, Mrs. Page," I repeated more loudly.

The noise didn't stop. Something seemed to snap inside me.

"For Christ's sake, Mrs. Page, shut your mouth," I shouted.

The wailing stopped abruptly. Mrs. Page had never been spoken to by a doctor like that before. In her book doctors were always gentlemen, mildly spoken and kind. She had manipulated them for years, and to be shouted at like that, well it really was too much. A look of horror and incomprehension flitted across her face. She looked like a spaniel puppy which has just been whipped. I felt sorry for her, but I didn't want to lose the upper hand now that I had it.

"That's better," I said. "There's no need for hysteria. He's only got a bruised toe."

Mrs. Page didn't make any reply at first. Then she opened her mouth and I thought I was going to hear some words of regret about the fuss she had made. But the only sound which came out was a weird croak, something between the caw of a crow and the sound of a rusty gate hinge.

"What's the matter?" I asked.

She shook her head and pointed to her mouth. I took out my pen torch and looked down her throat. Everything looked normal.

"Your voice gone, has it?" I said fatuously.

She nodded and I smiled. The situation was certainly novel and it had its bonus points. Mr. Page, I was certain, would be very appreciative of the rest.

"I expect it's all that howling," I said. "It will come back in due course. Perhaps you could bring John down to see me in the surgery in a couple of days' time and I'll have another look at that toe."

She nodded and I beat a hasty retreat.

When Mrs. Page brought John to the surgery that Friday, his toe was almost completely healed. But his mother still hadn't got her voice back. Nor had she a week later, nor the week after that. And every time I saw Mrs. Page she gave me a mute look of reproach which left me in no doubt that she blamed me for her disability.

After a month she still couldn't say a word, so I admitted defeat and referred her to the ENT Consultant in Angleton. He said there was nothing wrong with her vocal cords and her voice would soon return. Hysterical aphonia, he called it, but I think it was just plain old fashioned revenge.

24

The stench of cats was overpowering. Half eaten tins of cat food stood on the draining board of the kitchen sink and the lino covered floor was littered with dirty feeding bowls. Two of the animals had pushed their way past me as I had gone through the door and now three others hissed at me with their backs arched in hostility. One was perched precariously on the window sill, another on the table and the third on a wooden chair.

I didn't object to cats provided that they were properly looked after and tame, but these things were wild beasts.

"Why do you keep so many cats, Arthur?" I asked.

"Ter keep off them flyin' angels from next door," he replied.

"What flying angels?" I asked.

"Them Catholics next door send their flyin' angels round to torment us," said Arthur.

"Yes, flyin' angels," nodded Clarence like a puppet. "Flyin' angels from next door."

"But there aren't any flying angels," I said. "And even if there were, angels don't have the reputation for harming anyone."

"Don't yew believe it," said Arthur. "Yew aren't here at noight. Thass terrible."

I could see what the neighbours meant when they said that 'something ought to be done' about Clarence and Arthur. They were both mentally ill, but the question was, were they doing anybody any harm?

Not really, because this delusion about flying angels made them keep themselves very much to themselves. The only thing they wanted from their fellow human beings was the money from Social Security. When they had drawn that, they were quite happy with their cats and their fantasies. Once a week the grocery van called with the tins of cat food together with some human victuals, and you rarely saw the brothers out in daylight; they never went into the village shop. I suppose I was one of the few persons who was allowed into the house, but I didn't count it as any great privilege. Usually, I went at the request of Mrs. Cobbold, a non-Catholic neighbour who lived opposite the brothers and who relayed messages to the doctor for them. Mostly, I was asked to visit because of Arthur's bronchitis, but this time the message had been less specific. Both the brothers were reported to be 'goin' behind.' And now that I had set eyes on them I knew what Mrs. Cobbold had meant. The pair of them looked very thin and undernourished. The cats looked a lot better fed than they did, and if somebody didn't do something to help them they would probably soon succumb to some infective illness like pneumonia. I tried to veer the subject away from flying angels.

"How are you both keeping?" I asked.

"Orl roight," replied Arthur.

"What have you been eating?" I said.

"Onion puds," said Clarence. "They're lovely. Oi was makin' one just before yew came."

"Show me then," I said.

He was only too pleased to do so. He pushed one of the cats off the table and it scuttled into the living room. Then he took up a lump of dirty looking dough which the cat had just walked on and rolled it into a ball. He picked a filthy linen rag off the draining board of the sink and spread it out on the table. The dough was plonked unceremoniously on the rag and kneeded out into a pancake shape. A peeled raw onion was put in the centre of the pancake and then the dough and linen rag were brought up round the onion so they made a sort of bag, the mouth of which he tied with a bit of string. Clarence grinned at me and then shuffled over to the electric cooker and dunked the whole pudding in a pan of water. He tied the ends of the string round a wooden spoon which he balanced over the pan and switched on the electricity.

178

The job completed, he turned round and winked at me as though he was Robert Carrier and had just shown me a thing or two.

"They takes about twenty minutes," he said.

"I see," I said. "And what have you been having besides onion puddings?"

"Nothin' much," he said. "A bit of bread and butter chancetoime."

The cooking was certainly simplicity itself. It really didn't need a modern electric stove. A pan over any old hob would have done, and I expect that's exactly what they had had in their old cottage. The brothers had only been in this modern council bungalow for about four years. Before that they had lived in a broken down thatched cottage which was far more in keeping with their medieval lifestyle. But their hovel had blown down in a gale one night and the council had been forced to re-house them. Of course, the pair had done everything possible to make the new place seem like home — rags stuffed in broken window panes, piles of rubbish but no beds in the bedrooms and the cats allowed to roam everywhere. But it wasn't the same; especially with flying angels next door. And that's why they said they didn't have beds. It was too dangerous for them both to go to bed and sleep because of the risk of being attacked by flying angels, so at night the two of them took it in turns to have naps in the broken down old armchair which dominated the free space in their tiny sitting room.

When I had first visited them I had been very shocked. I had never seen anything like it before, and the initial impulse had been to 'do something'. But when I had realised that the two were doing nobody any harm I had decided that there was no need to do anything drastic like trying to get them admitted to a mental hospital. That had been some time ago, however; the situation had obviously deteriorated a great deal since then and they were in a far worse state than they had been on my last visit only a month before.

179

I looked down at Arthur's boots. Between where his trousers ended and his boots began I could see dirty bare flesh.

"Where are your socks, Arthur?" I asked.

"Never wear 'em," he said, and his long grey beard wagged as he talked. "They do wholly terrify me."

I now knew enough of the local dialect to be able to translate. He meant that socks made him itch. But seeing this little man standing there in his flat cap, dirty jacket and voluminous trousers held up by string, filled me with pity. The two just weren't being looked after properly, and they needed protecting from themselves.

"How about a spell in hospital," I said. "You both could do with a rest from all this trouble with the flying angels, and they would really feed you up."

"On onion puds?" asked Clarence. His Adam's apple moved up and down his scraggy neck as he talked and he reminded me of an emaciated turkey.

"Onion puds and other things too," I said.

Arthur looked doubtful.

"Any flyin' angels in hospital?" he asked.

"Not that I've heard of, or seen," I replied truthfully. I could see that Arthur was beginning to be attracted by the idea of going to hospital. The years of struggling against flying angels, of sitting up half the night and of living on Clarence's onion puddings had worn him down. Deep down, he knew he couldn't go on much longer as he had been doing.

"Come on," I said. "It would only be for a week or two." (I wasn't really so sure about that.)

"What about the cats?" asked Arthur.

I had already thought of that one.

"Oh, Mrs. Cobbold said she would see to them," I said. She had too, but only for a week or two. After that it would probably be another job for the RSPCA. But human lives were at stake. I couldn't be deflected from my purpose by a load of cats; especially those cats.

The brothers looked at me silently as they mulled the suggestion over. Their medical cards said that Arthur was sixty two and Clarence fifty six, but they could have been any age between forty five and ninety the pair of them. And as for belonging to the twentieth century, well they just didn't. Four hundred years ago they might have fitted in, but in this century they were anachronisms.

"Well, I can't stay here all day," I said. "What about it?"

"Orl roight," said Arthur.

"Orl roight," echoed Clarence.

"OK," I said. "I'll go and 'phone for the ambulance."

"An ambulance," said Clarence. "Do yew hear that Arthur? An ambulance. Oi've never bin in an ambulance afore."

I stepped outside and filled my lungs with fresh air as I walked down the short garden path. Mrs. Cobbold met me at the bottom of it.

"You're right," I said. "They really are going down hill, both physically and mentally. I've persuaded them to go into hospital, but only on condition that you look after the cats."

"Well, Oi told yew Oi'd do that," she said.

"Rather you than me," I replied. "You're not on the 'phone are you?"

"No, Oi have ter use the 'phone box," she said.

The telephone box was only about forty yards down the road. I walked down to it and 'phoned the mental hospital. The switchboard operator answered and I asked for the duty doctor.

"I'll try and find him," said the man. "I think I know where he is. If you give me your number I'll ring you back."

'That must mean the doctor's in the nurses' home or the pub,' I thought, but said nothing. I gave him my number and put the receiver down. I don't think the doctor had been in either of the places I had thought of because in a very few minutes the bell rang and a very sober sounding Indian voice was on the other end of the 'phone.

"Oh dear me," he said when I had told him the story. "Yes, it does sound as if they had better come in, sir," (I liked that.) "But two for the price of one, it's er . . ."

"Well it's no good sending one without the other," I said. "They're completely interdependent. I think if I left either one of them at home it would be the death of him in a very short time."

"Whatever you say, then," he said. "Can I have their names and ages please?"

I breathed a sigh of relief and told him what he wanted to know. When I had finished talking to him I put the receiver down, then picked it up again to telephone for the ambulance. As soon as I had finished that task I walked back up the street to the brothers' house, I saw several neighbours' curtains move as I did so. There was no doubt that I was under surveillance and I expect the hostile natives would give a cheer when they saw my two patients moving out. Among the lot of them only Mrs. Cobbold was being a real Christian and doing something positive to help. I met her at the gate again.

"I've fixed it up," I said. "It wasn't easy I can tell you. They don't like taking them two at a time."

Her face showed relief.

"Well, Oi'm glad, anyway," she said. "Poor souls, perhaps they'll get some proper attention now."

"Oh I'm sure they'll do their best in hospital," I said. "But I expect the brothers will get separated, and that won't be a good thing. Still, it will be off our plates anyway."

"Yes it will," she agreed.

I went back into the house. The stench of cat was only modified slightly by the lingering aroma of onion pudding. The brothers had had time to eat while I had been out.

"Is the ambulance here yet?" asked Clarence. He was really excited at the thought of the ambulance ride. I wondered if he had ever been in a motor car, or even out of the village.

"No, it will be a little while yet," I said. "I've got to write a letter to the hospital. Would you like to get a few things together while you wait."

"What things?" asked Arthur.

I was about to say pyjamas, toothbrush and a change of clothing when I remembered that neither of them had any of these possessions.

"Oh it doesn't matter," I said.

I took out a pen and pad and wrote a note to the duty psychiatrist. I had decided to wait for the ambulance to come, because I didn't want the brothers changing their minds at the last minute if I could help it. So when I had finished the letter I sealed it in an envelope and put it in my pocket.

"I'll tell the police you've gone into hospital," I said. "But perhaps you could leave the key with Mrs. Cobbold."

They agreed to do so.

I went and waited outside. The air was sweeter there. I chatted to Mrs. Cobbold for a few minutes and then we saw the ambulance turn the corner into the street.

The brothers weren't any trouble going off. Clarence was quite excited, but Arthur was only glumly cooperative.

They were loaded up, I handed one of the ambulancemen my letter, and then they were gone.

As the ambulance turned the corner again and disappeared out of sight I wondered if I would ever see those funny little men again. My guess was that they had eaten their last home-made onion pudding, and as it turned out my guess was correct. They both ended their days in the hospital.

25

"Hello, is that you, Doctor?" said a well spoken voice at the other end of the telephone.

"Yes, it is," I replied.

"Sorry to bother you out of hours but this is Mrs. Mole speaking. You know me, don't you? I organise the Meals on Wheels for Garham."

A vision of a motherly middle-aged lady with hornrimmed glasses floated in front of my eyes.

"Yes, I remember. We met when I gave those Red Cross lectures, didn't we."

"That's right," she said. "Well, I'm ringing you now because we have a few spare dinners going and someone suggested that William Tricker would benefit. I said I would ask you what you thought."

"I really don't know," I said. "I haven't seen him for ages. He doesn't bother me much. But I'll tell you what though. I've got to go to Garham tomorrow. I'll pop in and ask him what he thinks of the idea."

"Oh would you," she said. "I'd be very grateful. Some of these old people are so funny about having us, but they seem to accept the idea a lot more readily if the suggestion comes from the doctor."

"I agree," I said. "And it's no trouble at all. You ladies do a grand job you know, and I'm pleased to help if I can."

"It's nice of you to say so, Doctor," she said.

We said goodbye. As I put the receiver down, I wondered if my flattery had sounded convincing. It should have done, because I really believed what I had said. The women spent a lot of time and used a lot of their own petrol in making sure that the old people had this service, and because it was voluntary it was a lot more efficient than anything 'official' would have been. I sometimes wished that the NHS ran as smoothly as the Meals on Wheels Service.

The next day I put William Tricker on my visiting list as I had promised. The old boy had had a prostatectomy about eighteen months before, but since that time he hadn't troubled me much. The only times I had seen him in the last few months were when I had driven through the village and given him a wave as he had worked in his garden.

William was an old bachelor and he lived with his nephew Rufus. Rufus was unmarried too, and their council house was kept in a degree of medieval squalour which I had come to accept as the norm in such households. The nephew was twenty years younger than his uncle. He had a factory job in Angleton, but his chief claim to fame in Garham was as a follower of the local hunt. He was obsessed by it. On Meet days he would play hookey from work and whoop round the countryside on his bicycle. His sporting gear was almost as distinctive as the huntsmen's. It consisted of maroon coloured corduroy trousers, a green tweed jacket, a blue and white scarf and a bobble hat in the same colours.

The hunting fraternity regarded him as a mascot and the master had been known to delay the start of the Meet if Rufus hadn't arrived.

My only medical brush with the hunting fanatic had been when I had been called to see him because he had bronchitis. I examined him, wrote out a certificate and told him there would be some tablets and medicine to be collected from the surgery later that afternoon. Garham was full of Trickers, and in due course Rufus's fifteen year old nephew Tommy cycled up to Tunford. He parked his bike against the surgery wall and bounced in to see Mr. Somerville at the dispensary hatch.

"Oi've come fer Uncle Roo's medicine," he announced.

"Who's Uncle Roo?" asked Mr. Somerville, who wasn't on Christian name terms with Mr. Tricker.

"Uncle Roo's Uncle Roo," said the lad no doubt thinking how slow our dispenser was on the uptake.

"What's his surname though?" persisted Mr. Somerville.

"Uncle Roo," came back the reply.

"Uncle Roo who?"

"Uncle Roo."

Mr. Somerville realised that the boy just didn't know his Uncle's surname. He rang through to me.

"Who's Uncle Roo?" he asked.

"Rufus Tricker," I replied, putting an end to the mystery.

*

As far as I know, when he was younger William Tricker might have been just as enthusiastic in following the hunt as was Rufus, but he had slowed up a lot of late and nowadays he spent most of his time pottering about the garden when it was fine or huddling over the fire in the kitchen when it was not.

There was life in the old dog yet, though. He enjoyed reading 'Reveille' and 'Tit Bits' and he positively slavered over the Girlie pictures. But the poor old boy was deaf as a post despite his hearing aid, and I knew that I would have difficulty in getting through to him when I went to discuss the Meals on Wheels.

There was another problem too. He was very independent and I reckoned that he would think Meals on Wheels smacked of charity. I didn't really expect all that good a reception, and one way or another I had quite a flutter of anxiety in my chest as I pulled up outside the Trickers' gate. I walked up the well-worn dirt path and round to the back door. (I don't think anybody had been through the front door for twenty years.) The dog barked its head off and made an attempt to go for me, but it was tied to its kennel and I kept well outside the length of the chain. I opened the back door and went into the kitchen. Nobody was there, but a copy of 'Tit Bits' lay on the table.

'He must be in the back garden,' I thought. I went outside the house and shouted, but there was no reply except from the dog. The back garden was all of forty yards long and about half-way down was a wooden shed. The land was pretty overgrown, and there wasn't much to delight the eye of even a moderately keen horticulturalist like myself. I was about to turn away in disgust when I heard someone cough behind the shed. I walked down the path. William was certainly there but he hadn't been hiding. He just hadn't heard me. When I came up to him he was busy urinating on the rhubarb and he didn't seem at all put about when he saw me.

"Morning," I shouted.

"Mornin'," he replied. "Oi didn't send fer yew. What do yew want?"

He continued urinating. I noted that the stream was quite good. The prostatectomy had obviously been a lasting success.

"I've come about Meals on Wheels," I shouted in his ear.

"What?"

"Meals on Wheels," I yelled, getting closer. "You know, meals delivered to you. Like Mr. Frost over the road has. Somebody said you might like them."

"Loike hell Oi would," he said. "What would Oi need them fer?"

"I just thought you might like some addition to you diet."

"What for? Oi git plenty o' grub. An' don't shout so. Look, yew've made me piddle on me trousers."

26

I knew before Mrs. Runbelow opened her mouth that there was something else.

"Well, what is it?" I asked with a sigh as I walked into the waiting room. The place had just been cleared. It had been a long, hot evening surgery and I was dying for a glass of beer.

"Horace Rossington wants a visit," she said. "Number thirteen, The Street, Garham."

"I know the address well enough," I said. "I think I could find my way there in my sleep. What's wrong with him now?"

The mirage of the beer had disappeared completely.

"Well, his son rang," she replied. "He just said his Dad wasn't well and could the doctor please call."

"Couldn't it have waited until morning?" I asked.

"No, I'm afraid not. He wants to see you this evening."

"Typical," I said. "I expect he'll only have a cold or something when I get there. They really are a pest, those Rossingtons. I bet they wouldn't treat us like they do if they had to pay for our services."

Mrs. Runbelow smiled and waited for the storm to pass. She knew I would go in the end whatever I said. It was just too risky not to.

"Have you got the notes then?" I asked.

She handed them to me.

"Thanks," I said without much grace and slammed out through the door into the street.

Horace Rossington was a frail, anxiety ridden man of sixty five who didn't seem able to make the simplest decisions in life without consulting a doctor. He lived with his son Neville in a council house in Garham. I had never known Mrs. Rossington because she had died of cancer of the breast before I had arrived in Tunford, but I think she must have ruled the roost, because the domestic routine had certainly fallen apart since Neville and his father had been left on their own. In my opinion Neville was more of a hindrance to his father than a help. He had a factory job in Angleton, but he spent most of the time 'on the club' with a bad back. He tried to lean on his father, but his father just wasn't capable of being leant upon.

Horace found that life was altogether too much for him; he just hadn't got what it takes to cope. And as a result, he frequently paraded in the surgery with a physical symptom to justify his attendance. Ever since I had arrived in Tunford I had been seeing him on account of dry throats, tickly coughs, tingling in his feet, indigestion and insomnia. You name a symptom and Horace had had it. But numerous examinations and investigations had revealed no abnormality, and I must admit that these days I tended to reach for the pad and scribble a prescription for a tranquilliser before he even had a chance to sit down. My mind was closed to the possibility that he could produce a real physical illness. So you can imagine what an imposition it was to have to go and see him at home right after evening surgery.

And especially this evening, because Frances had invited Nigel and Patricia Childers to have dinner with us. The Childers were a young couple who had been on our table at the Rugby Club Ball. Nigel didn't play Rugby — he suffered from asthma, he said, but we had thought we would like to get to know him and his wife a bit better. They had a farm on the other side of Angleton, and we thought their talk was pleasantly non-medical. This was the first time the couple had been asked to our small flat and although I was on duty I had hoped that I wouldn't be called out. After all, it was high summer, and we expected to be slack at this time of year. But already it looked as if my luck wasn't going to hold. I climbed into my car and drove off towards Garham. The fields on either side of the road swayed with ripening corn and the countryside really looked beautiful.

You could see for miles; right over to Marsworth windmill on the horizon. If you forgot the occasional electricity pylon, you could have been looking at something straight out of a Constable painting, but I was in no mood to appreciate it.

That was the trouble with my job. We lived in the country, but I always seemed to be too busy or preoccupied to take any real account of the natural beauty around me.

When I arrived in Garham a group of children were playing on the green outside Horace's council house.

"Hello, Doctor," they shouted in unison as I stopped my car and got out.

"Hello," I replied. 'How nice to be that age again,' I thought. I dived into the Rossingtons' gateway and round to the back door. It was locked — perhaps a sign of Horace's insecurity. I knocked and presently Neville answered the door with a cigarette in his mouth.

"Evening," I said. "What's the matter with your Dad?"

"Oi dunno," he said, the cigarette moving with his speech. "He's upstairs."

Well, that was something. If he was in bed already it wouldn't take me long to examine him.

Neville stood aside and I brushed past him to go upstairs. As I did so he went back into the living room and I heard the volume of 'Coronation Street' being turned up on the television. I walked straight into Horace's bedroom.

"What's the matter?" I asked, not very kindly.

"Oi just feel awful, Doctor," he replied.

"Anything specific? Sore throat? Headache?"

"Moi throat's always droi. Yew know that."

I did.

"Any cough?"

"Well, Oi allus have a bit of a tissic."

"Yes, but are you bringing up any phlegm?"

"Not a lot."

"What colour is it when you do?"

"Clear whoite."

"What about the stomach?"

"Oi've had some indigestion, but no more than usual."

"Bowels OK?"

"Pardon?"

I was forgetting myself. The word 'bowel' didn't seem to be in the dictionary of a lot of the locals.

"Did you pass a motion today?"

"Yes," he said.

"And your waterworks. How are they?"

"Well Oi'm not the man Oi was, but . . ."

"Yes, but there's no pain when you pass water?"

"No."

I took his temperature. It was ninety nine degrees Fahrenheit. Horace looked at me quizzically as I read the scale.

"Yes, it is slightly up," I said. "But nothing to write home about."

I did a fairly thorough physical examination but found nothing abnormal.

"I expect it's a summer cold," I said when I had finished. "Stay where you are, drink plenty of fluids, and let me know if you don't feel a lot better in forty eight hours."

Horace didn't seem too satisfied.

"Aren't yew goin' ter give me any physic, Doctor?" he asked.

"No," I replied. "I don't think it's necessary."

I snapped my bag shut and stamped out of the house. Neville didn't hear me go. The television was going full blast.

The children who had been on the green were now playing around my car.

"Keep out of my way as I turn, won't you," I growled at them as I climbed into the vehicle. They saw I was in a bad temper and readily did what I asked. I wrenched the car round and drove off in a right old paddy. I thought Horace could well have put up with his symptoms until the morning. I reckoned he wouldn't have had me out if he had had to pay me five quid.

The National Health Service made it far too easy for patients to treat us like the tap water. Turn us on and we were there, just like that. And at any time it pleased them, day or night.

When I reached Tunford I parked the car in the street outside the flat as usual.

"Oh, hello dear," said Frances with relief in her voice as I walked in. Nigel and Pat had already arrived and I expect she had been finding it hard to play the hostess at the same time as keeping her eye on the cooking.

"Hello, everyone," I said. "Sorry I'm late. Just had a stupid call. The white man's burden and all that. Everyone got a drink?"

They had, so I helped myself to a beer. I had been thinking about that beer for a good two hours now, and my goodness it tasted good. I normally had a fairly strict rule about not drinking when I was on duty, but I didn't think a pint would do much harm. Anyway, I felt I had earned it. I settled down in an armchair and started to chat to our guests while Frances went off and busied herself in the kitchen.

The Childers really were a pleasant couple and Pat was a corker to look at. She had long fair hair with a gloss on it which would have done justice to a T.V. commercial, and when she smiled she displayed beautiful pearly white teeth. I tried to get her to smile as often as I could, but in doing so I discovered that as far as I was concerned she had a flaw. She was a bit of a prude and some of my usual anecdotes were obviously just a little too near the bone for her.

After ten minutes or so Frances came back into the room and announced that the food was ready. I excused myself to wash my hands and when I came back we went into our small dining room and sat down. With four of us sitting down at our table it was a bit like when Frank, Reuben and myself had been crushed up in the tractor cab, but at least it was intimate.

We started with sliced melon, and I had just about taken my first mouthful when the telephone rang.

"Blast," I said. "Excuse me won't you."

We didn't have a downstairs telephone extension in the flat, so I had to go upstairs to answer it.

I picked up the receiver and heard some pips and then a clunk as button A was pressed. It was Neville Rossington on the other end.

"Me father says 'e's worse," he said. "Can yew come roight away?"

It was very tempting to say "Stuff it," but my conscience wouldn't let me.

"Yes," I said between gritted teeth. "I'll come, but he'd better be ill this time, or else."

I slammed the receiver down and went back to our dinner party. "It's that old bugger Rossington," I said, mainly to my wife. "I've got to go out again, and I know before I go that there's damn all wrong with him."

I was seething, and the Childers looked very shocked. This wasn't the television image of a dedicated young doctor. There was obviously no Dr. Kildare or Dr. Finlay living in this house.

"Shall we wait for you after the first course?" asked Frances.

"No," I said. "You just carry on. Keep mine for me and I'll have it later."

I stormed out of the house. It was lucky the Garham road was clear. I drove along it like a madman; when I reached the Rossington residence I could barely wait for Neville to answer the back door. As soon as he did I grunted at him and stomped up the stairs. Horace didn't look much different.

"What is it now," I snarled like an Obersturmbannführer from the Gestapo.

"Oi just feel worse," he said.

"Is that all you can say," I said. "I drive out here to see you for the second time in an evening and you still can't produce any symptoms. Are you soft in the head or something? What's the matter with you man?"

"That's what Oi want yew ter tell me, Doctor," said Horace.

193

My temper collapsed like a pricked balloon.

"All right. Let's go through it again," I said. "In what way are you feeling ill?"

I repeated my history-taking and examination, but I didn't turn up anything fresh.

"Look," I said when I had finished. "You've got nothing much the matter with you that nature won't cure. Just a slight fever, that's all." I handed him some Paracetamol tablets from my bag. "Take two of these every four hours and drink lots of fluids. I'll be in to see you in the morning."

'That should do it,' I thought. 'The promise of a visit the next day should keep him quiet for the night anyway.'

I was down the stairs and out of the house in two shakes of a lamb's tail. When I got home again I found that the party had gone flat and my image remained a little tarnished. But I tried to recoup my losses. I ate my Lasagne while the others had their coffee meringue. They had left me a little red wine and I had a glass. I tried hard to tell some more funny stories, but somehow they didn't seem all that funny to the Childers. I caught up on the courses and eventually we all moved through to the sitting room for coffee. I kept up the stories and Pat Childers began to smile weakly at one or two of them. I began to feel my efforts were bearing fruit. She really did have lovely teeth. But the smile froze on her face when the telephone rang again. It was about ten o'clock.

"Oh no," I groaned, and then went off to answer it.

"That's Neville Rossington here," said the familiar voice at the other end of the line. "Father says he's sorry but he don't feel roight. Can yew come agin' please?"

I really lost my temper.

"I don't know what the hell he expects me to do," I shouted. "It's only a virus infection you know. But if he really wants me to come, yes I'll come."

I slammed the receiver down again.

"Would you believe it?" I said when I went back into the

sitting room. "The old sod wants me to visit again. Who'd be a bloody doctor?"

Our guests looked pale. I was so angry I think I scared them. They obviously couldn't believe that this sort of thing went on in doctors' households.

'Poor Frances,' I could imagine Pat Childers thinking. 'I wonder if he's a wife beater too? And such a foul tongue on him. His language would be more fitting on the dust cart.'

Frances tried to signal to me to shut up, but it was no use; I was too far gone in wrath to take any notice. I fumed out of the house muttering all sorts of obscenities to myself.

The car got punished again and I nearly stuck my head in Neville's stomach when he opened the back door of the house and I charged in. I climbed the stairs two at a time.

"What the . . ." I said as I burst into Horace's bedroom. But the words froze on my lips. The old boy looked terrible. His face was ashen grey and his forehead was covered in beads of sweat. I took his pulse and it was going nineteen to the dozen.

"Oi've got this terrible pain in me stomach," he said. I laid a hand on his abdomen. It was rock hard.

"Any pain in your shoulders?" I asked.

"Yes," he said.

Of course, that was it — a perforated peptic ulcer. Thank God I had come. But who would have thought it? He had had indigestion for some time, of course, but it had only been one of his many symptoms. Horace had been such a complainer that I just would never have believed that he could produce something genuine.

"I think you've burst an ulcer," I said.

He nodded. He knew he was sick all right. Hadn't he been trying to tell me that all evening?

"You'll have to go into hospital," I said.

Horace nodded again. He knew that too.

"I'll go and 'phone the ambulance," I said. "I'm very sorry, but you had no signs before. I just couldn't fathom it."

195

"Tha's orl roight, Doc," he said. "Yew kept comin', anyway," he replied.

I went downstairs. Neville got up from the television as I walked into the sitting room. He had another cigarette in his mouth.

"Your father's perforated a stomach ulcer," I said. "He'll have to go into hospital for an operation."

"Oh yes," said Neville. "And when will he hev this operation?"

"As soon as possible," I said. "If the hole in the wall of his stomach isn't sewn up, he'll die of peritonitis."

"Oi thought he was queer," said Neville, scratching his head.

I left the house and went across to the village telephone kiosk to make all the necessary arrangements. When I had done that I went back to Horace and wrote a letter to the surgical houseman. I gave the letter to the patient and then once more headed for home. The ambulance would be along in a very few minutes. I drove back to Tunford in a very rueful mood. Life in general practice certainly wasn't easy; it was full of pitfalls for the unwary. On the first two visits to Horace I must have missed something. To be honest I had really only gone through the motions of taking a history and examining him. And why? Because I had been in a filthy mood. I really would have to control myself. Why couldn't I be more phlegmatic like Timothy Bacon? He wouldn't have flown of the handle like that.

But it was a good job that we had that unwritten rule about always visiting when we were asked to. If I hadn't obeyed it this time I might have been in deep trouble. And that was the only thing I could congratulate myself on. At least I had gone.

So had our visitors when I got home.

"I don't think we'll see Nigel and Pat again," said Frances. "I'm afraid you shocked them to the core."

"I'm sorry I lost my temper," I said. "I feel terrible about it now because the old boy had a perforated ulcer."

"It's a good job you went, then," she said.

"You're right," I said. "But about our visitors. I don't think we should try to entertain people when I'm on duty, do you?"

"No," she said. "It doesn't exactly improve their opinion of doctors."

"What's your opinion of doctors?" I asked.

"Slobs," she said, and I grabbed her in my arms and kissed her.

She responded warmly, and for the first time I got the impression that the evening was at last taking a turn for the better.

27

"How are young Jonathan's beans then, Arthur?" asked Daisy Woodcock with a crafty wink in my direction.

Arthur Hambling smiled and I watched the expression on his face change with much the same pleasure as a holidaymaker when he sees the sun break from behind the clouds.

A retired gamekeeper, Arthur suffered from arthritis of the hips. He was on the waiting list to have an operation at the Angleton Hospital but his name hadn't come up yet. Meanwhile, he found it a lot easier to cycle than to walk and the half mile bike ride from his cottage to the Three Tuns was often accomplished.

Daisy treated Arthur with the same practised sympathy with which she treated all her regular customers (those she liked anyway) and I'm sure even a trained psychotherapist could have learnt a lot from her. She was I suppose Tunford's answer to the geisha girl, though the thought of her in a kimono performing a tea ceremony was rather comic. Nevertheless, I often told her that she did a lot more good than I did and she deserved a subsidy from the Department of Health for her services to the community.

Arthur was like the rest of us. He came to have his morale boosted and to hear the gossip. But the process wasn't all one way. He himself had a fund of stories to tell and I always enjoyed having a chat with him. Of late, the old gamekeeper's most amusing tales had been about his neighbour Jonathan, who was another of Daisy's customers.

Jonathan was a bachelor who had a small cottage with a quarter of an acre of land right next to Arthur's place. I liked the lad. He was a young journalist who saw a bright future for himself in the media. He had no intention at all of spending the next thirty years rotting in Tunford. No indeed, for him the future path would lead him far away and ever upwards. At present he was only writing the agricultural column in the local paper, but he had every intention of getting into television and thence perhaps into Parliament. He didn't understand me at all, for I had developed into a real stay-at-home villager.

I had tried to explain to him why I wanted to remain where I was. I had been in Tunford for nearly three years now and London seemed like a distant nightmare. It was true that general practice in the country wasn't half so easy as I had thought it was going to be. At times the workload was almost intolerable and I often had difficulty in controlling my anger and sense of frustration when things really got on top of me. But the battle with my own personality had been somewhat therapeutic and I felt that I had come to know myself better. The job had become far more satisfying now that people were getting to know me and beginning to have some confidence in me. The way I had chosen wasn't easy but it had great compensations. Timothy and I still had a very good relationship and I thought that our ideals and standards of practice were high. The only regret I had was that we still worked from very primitive premises, but as an ex-missionary doctor had once pointed out to me, you can do some pretty good things for humanity in a mud hut if the will is there.

Despite the careful exposition of my philosophy on numerous occasions in the Three Tuns, Jonathan still didn't understand me. But I understood him all right. He was unmarried and unlike me he didn't have a wife far advanced in her second pregnancy. To him Tunford must have seemed a dull place and I could sympathise with his thrusting desire to move away and get on in the world.

But for my part I hoped that as I grew older I would learn to cope with life as well as Daisy and some of her regulars. Arthur, for instance, had a lot to be miserable about. He was a widower, his cottage was small and lacking in almost every modern convenience and his sole income was the Old Age pension. But if anyone had discovered the secret to life it was Arthur Hambling. He took pleasure in simple things and seemed incredibly satisfied with the little he had. In attitude he was poles apart from his neighbour Jonathan and it was hardly surprising that like most of the customers of the Three Tuns he regarded the journalist as a young whipper-snapper who had a lot to learn.

Everyone who drank in the pub regularly was well aware that Jonathan used the place as a source of ideas when he was short of copy. The farmers were not at all afraid of capitalising on this fact and would tell the naive budding writer the tallest of stories which he often swallowed hook, line and sinker. Headlines like 'Best Beet Crop in Tunford for Thirty Years' or 'Plague of Rats Eat Tunford Farmers' Profits' were a regular occurrence and there was a right old scramble to read what 'squit' our Jonathan had written when the Angleton News reached the Three Tuns every Friday.

But when the agricultural stories were scarce the journalist really had to scratch around to fill his column. So much so that he would sometimes descend to writing about his own horticultural efforts in his cottage garden. This was a mistake, because although only a small proportion of the population of Tunford could reckon themselves to be agricultural experts, nearly everybody had a garden and took a keen interest in it.

And none was more interested in gardening than Arthur Hambling. It was a pity that his arthritis of the hips restricted him so, but it was no doubt that which made him more of a watcher than a doer. He watched Jonathan's garden with a very keen eye indeed and he regularly reported his observations back to the Three Tuns. His comments so far had been quite caustic, especially when the young journalist had put some 'bag muck' on his runner beans. But the beans had survived the treatment and had already been mentioned once or twice in the weekly newspaper column. The whole of Tunford had been waiting for more.

Arthur put his pint pot down on the table in front of him in a very deliberate fashion. It had seemed an age since Daisy had asked her question but it was probably only a second or two in reality. He had obviously been searching around in his mind for the necessary words with which to describe Jonathan's scarlet runners.

"Oi'm not the man Oi was yew know," he said. "But Oi tell yew Oi could pee the height o' them beans."

28

I wrote 'Condoms please' on a piece of paper and handed it to the girl.

"Now take this over to Mr. Bailey at the shop," I said. "He and I have an arrangement over these things and he will let you have the goods in a plain wrapper."

"Thank yew, doctor," she said, her face flushing slightly as she took the paper from me and discreetly folded it twice.

I wasn't corrupting anyone's morals. This girl and her boyfriend had been having unprotected intercourse for some weeks, and I was only giving what I thought was sensible advice. For several months I had been pressing Timothy and Mr. Somerville to allow the sale of condoms at the dispensary, but there had been some reluctance. I could understand it on Timothy's part. It would look a bit funny if he got the name for being a purveyor of contraceptives while he was still a bachelor. But I reckoned that the problem of getting supplies of these things was a very real one to some people, despite the fact that Harry Bailey sold them. The difficulty was that there was little confidentiality in the grocer's shop, and people had a natural diffidence about asking for French letters over the counter. Some just couldn't face up to it, and that's why I had come up with this idea of 'prescriptions'. It had been hatched, as usual, in the Rugby Club bar, but this was the first time I had actually put it to the test.

As she left the consulting room I felt that at last I was becoming a good GP. People were confiding their little secrets to me and I was finding ways of helping them out. Not always orthodox, to be sure, but that pleased me too. I was using my initiative.

I continued with my surgery and my nineteen year old

patient did as I had told her to and went across the road to see Harry Bailey.

But it was a bad day for Harry. School holidays nearly always did cause bad days in the grocer's shop. There had been a lot of children in with sixpences to spend, and a lot more with little notes from their mothers saying things like:

> '1 lf Brd.
> Half doz eggs
> 1 pkt cheese bskts
> Pay on Friday'

He was feeling definitely peeved, and when my note was handed to him he thought it was nearly the last straw. The shop was full, and what's more he had temporarily misplaced his glasses. Harry snatched the piece of paper off my patient and tried unsuccessfully to read it at arm's length. He handed it back.

"I can't see what it says without me specs.," he said crossly. "You read it to me."

The girl went scarlet.

"Oi can't read it either," she blurted out. Then she screwed up the note, dropped it on the floor, turned and fled. Harry shrugged his shoulders and got on with serving the next customer.

Later that day he was cleaning up the shop after closing time when he came across my 'prescription'. Out of curiosity he unscrewed the bit of paper and deciphered the message. He telephoned me and told me what had happened.

"I'm awfully sorry, old chap," he said. "I hope it doesn't have any dire consequences."

"Never mind," I said. "It can't be helped. If she has a boy I'll suggest that she calls him Harry."

But although I had made a joke of it, inwardly I wasn't very pleased at all. The very next day I tackled Timothy and Mr. Somerville again.

"It's all very well in the towns," I said. "There are no end of

203

chemists selling French letters. But out here it's different; even some of the married people are too shy to go to Harry Bailey. Couldn't we just have a few of the things to sell in emergencies? We could always give them an address to get their follow-up supplies by post."

"Oh all right," said Timothy. "I'm rather sick of hearing about it, aren't you Mr. Somerville?"

"Well, er, yes," said Mr. Somerville.

Victory was mine; I went off on my calls a happier man.

*

As I had predicted, when we introduced our new contraceptive service we weren't overwhelmed, but I did find it very useful to be able to hand the women a 'starter pack' at their post-natal examination and occasionally I would sell them to an unmarried person whom I knew to be at risk. But history shows that all revolutions have a tendency to backfire on their perpetrators, and the Tunford Contraceptive Revolution was no exception.

One Saturday morning several weeks after we had begun to sell the items in question I was driving around on my calls. Life was going quite well just then. We weren't particularly busy in the practice and there had been more time to relax. To add to my comfort, I had just that morning learned that I had won £5 in the Tunford Cricket Club draw. It wasn't a vast amount but it should see me right for a few jars in the Three Tuns that lunchtime. The sun was shining and the inside of the car was warm. I normally kept wide awake when I was driving but that morning I was a bit dopey. It was like going to sleep in the bath. Suddenly you wake up to find that the water's cold. Well, I woke up to find that I had nearly driven past the council house I was supposed to be visiting. I put on the brakes and stopped precipitately. To my surprise, there was a screech of brakes to my rear and a little green van scraped past me and came to a halt just in front. He must have been following close behind but

I hadn't seen him in the driving mirror. To be honest I don't think I had looked. The driver got out. He looked pretty wild with me and I thought he was about to tear me apart. I had to admit to myself that my driving hadn't been very careful but nobody had come to any harm and neither vehicle had been damaged. Why did he have to look so aggressive? But aggression was in this man's nature. I knew him well. It was Kevin Milligan, the bricklayer, husband of Kathleen Milligan who had had her fourth post-natal examination only a week before. I had given her a long overdue lecture on contraception, as well as some condoms as a free sample.

As he lumbered towards me I had to admit to myself that he was a fine figure of a man. His muscles were kept in trim by constant physical exercise and he looked and moved like a professional boxer. I knew that despite my Rugby training, if it came to a physical contest, in a few moments I would be lying on my back with half my teeth down my throat. I decided to try and talk my way out of it; say I was sorry but hadn't seen him; I had been up half the night and was tired out. The last bit was all lies but it might sound convincing.

I wound down the car window by about two inches — enough space to talk through but not enough to thump through. My potential adversary came up to the car, bent his body down from his six feet two inches and stuck his face next to mine.

With an exhalation of breath which I couldn't help noticing was sweetened with alcohol he said, "Got any more o' them French letters you gave me wife, Doc?"

29

"Have another drink," said the schoolmaster.

"I really don't think I should," said Frances. "I'm two days over already and I could end up in the Angleton General tonight you know. What would they think if I turned up drunk?"

"Two small gins won't make you drunk," said the sage.

"All right," she said. "But mind you make it a little one."

He went off to fill her glass and I gave her a wink. We liked Bill Maynard and his wife Marjorie and we hadn't liked to refuse the invitation to their party. Anyway, we needed cheering up. Frances was fed up with being pregnant and it was infectious. The party wasn't a bad one either. There was a handful of local dignitaries and people from the County Education department, it's true, but there were also several of my friends from the Rugby Club, and I had soon found my level.

"He's a devil when he gets going," I observed.

Frances agreed. "But I'm going to drink his gin, nevertheless," she said. "They say it can start you off sometimes, don't they?"

"I'm not so sure about that," I said. "But I hope so for your sake."

"Well, you'll take care to remain sober, won't you," she said. "You may have to drive me into Angleton later."

"Cross my heart," I said. "My limit's going to be two pints of beer. Oh hello, Andrew," I said. Andrew Drayton had just come up to chat with us. I admired him greatly. He was a very good flautist and my fiddle playing was as nothing in comparison.

"How's the flute?" I asked.

"Oh still playing," he said. "You know, we could get up a quartet sometime . . ."

The conversation drifted on and Frances moved away to

talk to Andrew's wife. I saw Bill Maynard give her her glass of gin and tonic, but after that she disappeared from my vision and the next thing I knew it was an hour and a half later and she was tapping me on the elbow.

"Come on," she said. "Have you seen the clock? It's midnight. Time you left the ball, Cinders."

"OK," I said, downing the remains of my second pint (I had been true to my word). "Better find Bill and Marjorie to thank them."

We did so.

"You're not going already, are you?" said Bill.

"Well, we don't want to, but I think we really must," I said. "Tonight could be the night, you know," I said patting Frances lightly on the abdomen. "Thanks for a super party, anyway."

"And the food was really marvellous, Marjorie," said Frances.

"Oh, thank you," said Marjorie. "It was a pleasure. I hope everything will go all right. That is, if I don't see you again before the event."

"Thank you," said Frances.

Bill showed us to the door. We said goodbye and crunched our way across Bill's gravel yard to where our car was parked. The night was cool and fresh and for once I was quite capable of driving home.

"That was a good do," I said as we climbed into the Morris, "but I think they were all a bit worried in case you went into labour right in the middle of the floor."

"No such luck," said Frances as I turned the ignition key and started the engine.

A quarter of an hour later we had dismissed the babysitter and we were safely tucked up in bed. I was soon off into a deep sleep, but at five o'clock in the morning Frances woke me.

"I'm having pains," she said.

"How often?" I asked.

"About every twenty minutes."

"The membranes haven't ruptured have they?"

"No," she replied.

"Well, try and get some sleep," I said. "It will be hours yet." I wasn't going to be one of those panicky sorts who rushed his wife off to hospital at the first pain; I rolled over and went to sleep again.

But at six o'clock she woke me up once more.

"The pains are a lot worse," she said.

"All right," I replied. "I'm getting up, but I don't think there's any hurry. You won't have it for hours yet."

I went off to the bathroom and had a fairly leisurely wash and shave. 'Never run,' my old professor had said. 'Take your time and everything will be all right.' I splashed on some after-shave and went back into the bedroom. Frances was sitting on the edge of the bed.

"I want to push," she said accusingly.

A sudden panic gripped me. What the hell was I going to do if she had it at home? It was all very well delivering other people's babies, but my own — never! Anyway she was booked for hospital. We didn't have a thing ready for a domiciliary confinement. And no son of mine was going to be born into the Eastern Daily Times.

"Good God," I said. "Why didn't you tell me sooner?"

"I did," she reminded me, "but you kept saying it was going to be hours yet."

"I'll give Jane a ring," I said. "We'll have to move fast."

With a shaking hand I picked up the 'phone. Our friend Jane Cockerton had promised to come and stay with Sally if Frances went into labour during the night. I dialled her number and she answered almost immediately.

"It's Corney here," I said. "Can you come quickly? Frances wants to push and I'm going to take her into Angleton straightaway."

"Right," said Jane. "I won't be long. But if I'm not there before you go, leave the door open so that I'll be able to walk straight in."

"Thanks very much," I said, and slammed the receiver down. I pulled my clothes on as quickly as I could.

"How do you feel now?" I asked.

"All right," she said. "No pain just at this moment. It's gone off."

"Here then," I said. "Put on your dressing gown and your slippers. And be quick won't you, love? I don't think we've got much time. Let's try and get you downstairs before you have another contraction."

She did as I had suggested and we reached the bottom of the stairs before another pain came.

"It's no use," she said. "I'll have to rest." She sat down on the bottom step.

"OK," I said. "You just stay there and take big breaths in and out. Don't push for God's sake. I'll get the car going."

I shot out of the door, unlocked the car, hopped in and turned the ignition key. The motor turned over but wouldn't start. I gave a little prayer and tried again. My prayer was answered. The engine coughed into life. I left it running with the choke out and went back to my wife. She was in between pains again.

"Come on," I said. "Just a few steps to the car."

I put my arm around her and helped her into the front passenger seat. I slammed the door behind her and then rushed round to my side and jumped in. I flung the machine into gear and let out the clutch. The engine stalled, and so nearly did my heart.

"Damn," I said. "Where's your nerve, Slater?"

I started the engine again and this time engaged the gears and let out the clutch without mishap. We careered off down the road.

Jane Cockerton rounded the street corner on her bicycle just as we left and I gave her a loud hoot on the horn. Goodness knows what the residents of Tunford would think about that, but I was past caring about them. I drove as if the devil himself was after me. Frances had another pain when we were half way to Angleton but I closed my ears to her. I wasn't going to stop unless she actually had the baby there and then, God forbid.

The road was clear, and eight minutes after we had left Tunford we were pulling up in the car park outside the maternity wing of the hospital.

"How do you feel?" I asked.

Her face was screwed up. Another pain had just started.

"I can't hold it much longer," she said.

"Oh God. Well try, won't you? I'll go and get some help," I said. I burst into the maternity unit and found the sister in her office. She recognised me and smiled.

"Now what obstetric drama is it this time, Dr. Slater?" she asked, remembering the delivery during a power cut.

"My wife's in the car and I think she's well into the second stage," I said. "Have you got a wheelchair?"

"Certainly," she replied. "There's one in the corner of the waiting room. I'll come and help you."

We collected the wheelchair and tore out to the car park at the double. Frances' pain was now almost continuous, but somehow the sister and I managed to get her into the chair. Then we propelled her into the labour ward as fast as we could. Sister and another midwife helped my wife onto the couch and suddenly I felt superfluous.

"I'll wait outside," I said. I blew a kiss to Frances, but I don't think she noticed. I had no desire to wait to see our baby being born. I had long got past the stage of thinking that childbirth was marvellous. To me, it was a dangerous, spine-chilling affair, and if my professional colleagues had to deal with anything nasty, they would work far better without my being there.

As I made my way down the corridor to the waiting room, the sister came out of the labour ward and went back into her office. I heard her telephoning Hector MacDonald.

"Oh Sister O'Neal here, sir," she said. "Dr. Slater's wife has come in and she's fully dilated. You said we were to let you know . . ."

Mr. MacDonald must have thanked her for the message.

"See you in a few minutes then, sir," she said, and put the receiver down. But as she left her office and pushed her way through the double swing doors of the labour room again I heard a baby cry. It looked as though Hector MacDonald was going to be too late. I stayed in the waiting room until Sister O'Neal came back to me. It seemed an age, but eventually she appeared at the door.

"You've got another little girl," she said.

"Thank God for that," I said. "Is Frances all right?"

"Yes, fine. She'll need a few stitches, but Mr. MacDonald will see to that when he arrives."

"That's splendid," I said. I wasn't at all disappointed that we hadn't had a boy. My predominant feeling was one of profound relief. We had made it to the hospital and everything was all right. I don't know what I would have done if I had been forced to cope with delivering the baby by myself in the flat, or even worse in the car. I think I would most probably have fainted. Hector arrived and after a few words with Sister O'Neal he came down to the waiting room to see me.

"You cut it fine," he said, beaming all over his face.

"Too right," I replied.